A STORY OF THE GOLDEN AGE
OF GREEK HEROES

A STORY OF THE GOLDEN AGE OF GREEK HEROES

BY

JAMES BALDWIN

YESTERDAY'S CLASSICS

CHAPEL HILL, NORTH CAROLINA

This edition, first published in 2006 by Yesterday's Classics, is an unabridged republication of the work originally published as *A Story of the Golden Age* by Charles Scribner's Sons in 1896. For a listing of books published by Yesterday's Classics, visit www.yesterdaysclassics.com. Yesterday's Classics is the publishing arm of the Baldwin Project which presents the complete text of dozens of classic books for children at www.mainlesson.com under the editorship of Lisa M. Ripperton and T. A. Roth.

ISBN-10: 1-59915-026-3

ISBN-13: 978-1-59915-026-0

Yesterday's Classics
PO Box 3418
Chapel Hill, NC 27515

TO MAY

THE FORE WORD

You have heard of Homer, and of the two wonderful poems, the Iliad and the Odyssey, which bear his name. No one knows whether these poems were composed by Homer, or whether they are the work of many different poets. And, in fact, it matters very little about their authorship. Everybody agrees that they are the grandest poems ever sung or written or read in this world; and yet, how few persons, comparatively, have read them, or know any thing about them except at second-hand! Homer commences his story, not at the beginning, but "in the midst of things;" hence, when one starts out to read the Iliad without having made some special preparation beforehand, he finds it hard to understand, and is tempted, in despair, to stop at the end of the first book. Many people are, therefore, content to admire the great masterpiece of poetry and story-telling simply because others admire it, and not because they have any personal acquaintance with it.

Now, it is not my purpose to give you a "simplified version" of the Iliad or the Odyssey. There are already many such versions; but the best way for you, or any one else, to read Homer, is *to read Homer.* If you do not understand Greek, you can read him in one of the many English translations.

You will find much of the spirit of the original in the translations by Bryant, by Lord Derby, and by old George Chapman, as well as in the admirable prose rendering by Butcher and Lang; but you can get none of it in any so-called simplified version.

My object in writing this "Story of the Golden Age" has been to pave the way, if I dare say it, to an enjoyable reading of Homer, either in translations or in the original. I have taken the various legends relating to the causes of the Trojan war, and, by assuming certain privileges never yet denied to story-tellers, have woven all into one continuous narrative, ending where Homer's story begins. The hero of the Odyssey—a character not always to be admired or commended—is my hero. And, in telling the story of his boyhood and youth, I have taken the opportunity to repeat, for your enjoyment, some of the most beautiful of the old Greek myths. If I have, now and then, given them a coloring slightly different from the original, you will remember that such is the right of the story-teller, the poet, and the artist. The essential features of the stories remain unchanged. I have, all along, drawn freely from the old tragedians, and now and then from Homer himself; nor have I thought it necessary in every instance to mention authorities, or to apologize for an occasional close imitation of some of the best translations. The pictures of old Greek life have, in the main, been derived from the Iliad and the Odyssey, and will, I hope, help you to a better understanding of those poems when you come to make acquaintance directly with them.

Should you become interested in the "Story of the Golden Age," as it is here related, do not be disappointed by its somewhat abrupt ending; for you will find it continued by the master-poet of all ages, in a manner both inimitable and unapproachable. If you are pleased with the discourse of the porter at the gate, how much greater shall be your delight when you stand in the palace of the king, and hearken to the song of the royal minstrel!

CONTENTS

CONTENTS

A GLIMPSE OF THE WORLD

To the simple-hearted folk who dwelt in that island three thousand years ago, there was never a sweeter spot than sea-girt Ithaca. Rocky and rugged though it may have seemed, yet it was indeed a smiling land embosomed in the laughing sea. There the air was always mild and pure, and balmy with the breath of blossoms; the sun looked kindly down from a cloudless sky, and storms seldom broke the quiet ripple of the waters which bathed the shores of that island home. On every side but one, the land rose straight up out of the deep sea to meet the feet of craggy hills and mountains crowned with woods. Between the heights were many narrow dells green with orchards; while the gentler slopes were covered with vineyards, and the steeps above them gave pasturage to flocks of long-wooled sheep and mountain-climbing goats.

On that side of the island which lay nearest the rising sun, there was a fine, deep harbor; for there the shore bent inward, and only a narrow neck of land lay between the eastern waters and the western sea. Close on either side of this harbor arose two mountains, Neritus and Nereius, which stood like giant watchmen overlooking land and sea and warding harm away; and on the neck, midway between these mountains, was the king's white palace, roomy and large, with blossoming orchards to the right and the left, and broad lawns in front, sloping down to the water's edge.

Here, many hundreds of years ago, lived Laertes—a man of simple habits, who thought his little island home a kingdom large enough, and never sighed for a greater. Not many men had seen so much of the world as he; for he had been to Colchis with Jason and the Argonauts, and his feet had trod the streets of every city in Hellas. Yet in all his wanderings he had seen no fairer land than rocky Ithaca. His eyes had been dazzled by the brightness of the Golden Fleece, and the kings of Argos and of Ilios had shown him the gold and gems of their treasure-houses. Yet what cared he for wealth other than that which his flocks and vineyards yielded him? There was hardly a day but that he might be seen in the fields guiding his plough, or training his vines, or in his orchards pruning his trees, or gathering the mellow fruit. He had all the good gifts of life that any man needs; and for them he never failed to thank the great Giver, nor to render praises to the powers above. His queen, fair Anticleia, daughter of the aged chief Autolycus, was a true housewife, overseeing the maidens at their tasks, busying herself with the distaff and the spindle, or plying the shuttle at the loom; and many were the garments, rich with finest needlework, which her own fair fingers had fashioned.

To Laertes and Anticleia one child had been born,—a son, who, they hoped, would live to bring renown to Ithaca. This boy, as he grew, became strong in body and mind far beyond his playfellows; and those who knew him wondered at the shrewdness of his speech no less than at the strength and suppleness of his limbs. And yet he was small of stature, and neither in face nor in figure was he adorned with any of Apollo's grace. On the day that he was twelve years old, he stood with his tutor, the bard Phemius, on the top of Mount Neritus; below him, spread out like a great map, lay what was to him the whole world. Northward, as far as his eyes could see, there were islands great and small; and among them Phemius pointed out Taphos, the home of a sea-faring race, where Anchialus, chief of warriors, ruled. Eastward were other isles, and the low-lying shores of Acarnania, so far away that they seemed mere lines of hazy green between the purple waters and the azure sky. Southward beyond Samos were the wooded heights of Zacynthus, and the sea-paths which led to Pylos and distant Crete. Westward was the great sea, stretching away and away to the region of the setting sun; the watery kingdom of Poseidon, full of strange beings and unknown dangers,—a sea upon which none but the bravest mariners dared launch their ships.

The boy had often looked upon these scenes of beauty and mystery, but to-day his heart was stirred with an unwonted feeling of awe and of wonder at the greatness and grandeur of the world as it thus lay around him. Tears filled his eyes as he turned to his tutor. "How kind it was of the Being who made this pleasant earth, to set our own sunny Ithaca right in the centre of it, and to cover it all over with a blue dome like a tent! But tell me, do people live in all those lands that we see? I know that there are men dwelling in Zacynthus and in the little islands of the eastern sea; for their fishermen often come to Ithaca, and I have talked with them. And I have heard my father tell of his wonderful voyage to Colchis, which is in the region of the rising sun; and my mother often speaks of her old home in Parnassus, which also is far away towards the dawn. Is it true that there are men, women, and children, living in lands which we cannot see? and do the great powers above us care for them as for the good people of Ithaca? And is there anywhere another king so great as my father Laertes, or another kingdom so rich and happy as his?"

Then Phemius told the lad all about the land of the Hellenes beyond the narrow sea; and, in the sand at their feet, he drew with a stick a map of all the countries known to him.

"We cannot see half of the world from this spot," said the bard, "neither is Ithaca the centre of it, as it seems to you. I will draw a picture of it here in the sand, and show you where lies every land and every sea. Right here in the very centre," said he, heaping up a pile of sand into the shape of a moun-

A GLIMPSE OF THE WORLD.

tain,—"right here in the very centre of the world is
Mount Parnassus, the home of the Muses; and in its
shadow is sacred Delphi, where stands Apollo's
temple. South of Parnassus is the Bay of Crissa,
sometimes called the Corinthian Gulf. The traveller
who sails westwardly through those waters will have
on his right hand the pleasant hills and dales of

5

Ætolia and the wooded lands of Calydon; while on his left will rise the rugged mountains of Achaia, and the gentler slopes of Elis. Here to the south of Elis are Messene, and sandy Pylos where godlike Nestor and his aged father Neleus reign. Here, to the east, is Arcadia, a land of green pastures and sweet contentment, unwashed by any sea; and next to it is Argolis,—rich in horses, but richest of all in noble men,—and Lacedæmon in Laconia, famous for its warriors and its beautiful women. Far to the north of Parnassus is Mount Olympus, the heaven-towering home of Zeus, and the place where the gods and goddesses hold their councils."

Then Phemius, as he was often wont to do, began to put his words into the form of music; and he sang a song of the world as he supposed it to be. He sang of Helios the Sun, and of his flaming chariot and his four white steeds, and of the wonderful journey which he makes every day above the earth; and he sang of the snowy mountains of Caucasus in the distant east; and of the gardens of the Hesperides even farther to the westward; and of the land of the Hyperboreans, which lies beyond the northern mountains; and of the sunny climes where live the Ethiopians, the farthest distant of all earth's dwellers. Then he sang of the flowing stream of Ocean which encircles all lands in its embrace; and, lastly, of the Islands of the Blest, where fair-haired Rhadamanthus rules, and where there is neither snow nor beating rains, but everlasting spring, and breezes balmy with the breath of life.

"O Phemius!" cried the boy, as the bard laid aside his harp, "I never knew that the world was so large. Can it be that there are so many countries and so many strange people beneath the same sky?"

"Yes," answered Phemius, "the world is very broad, and our Ithaca is but one of the smallest of a thousand lands upon which Helios smiles, as he makes his daily journey through the skies. It is not given to one man to know all these lands; and happiest is he whose only care is for his home, deeming it the centre around which the world is built."

"If only the half of what you have told me be true," said the boy, "I cannot rest until I have seen some of those strange lands, and learned more about the wonderful beings which live in them. I cannot bear to think of being always shut up within the narrow bounds of little Ithaca."

"My dear boy," said Phemius, laughing, "your mind has been greatly changed within the past few moments. When we came here, a little while ago, you thought that Neritus was the grandest mountain in the world, and that Ithaca was the centre round which the earth was built. Then you were cheerful and contented; but now you are restless and unhappy, because you have learned of possibilities such as, hitherto, you had not dreamed about. Your eyes have been opened to see and to know the world as it is, and you are no longer satisfied with that which Ithaca can give you."

"But why did you not tell me these things before?" asked the boy.

"It was your mother's wish," answered the bard, "that you should not know them until to-day. Do you remember what day this is?"

"It is my twelfth birthday. And I remember, too, that there was a promise made to my grandfather, that when I was twelve years old I should visit him in his strong halls on Mount Parnassus. I mean to ask my mother about it at once."

And without waiting for another word from Phemius, the lad ran hurriedly down the steep pathway, and was soon at the foot of the mountain. Across the fields he hastened, and through the vineyards where the vines, trained by his father's own hand, were already hanging heavy with grapes. He found his mother in the inner hall, sitting before the hearth, and twisting from her distaff threads of bright sea-purple, while her maidens plied their tasks around her. He knelt upon the marble floor, and gently clasped his mother's knees.

"Mother," he said, "I come to ask a long-promised boon of you."

"What is it, my son?" asked the queen, laying aside her distaff. "If there be any thing in Ithaca that I can give you, you shall surely have it."

"I want nothing in Ithaca," answered the boy; "I want to see more of this great world than I ever yet have known. And now that I am twelve years old, you surely will not forget the promise, long since made, that I should spend the summer with my grandfather at Parnassus. Let me go very soon, I pray; for I tire of this narrow Ithaca."

The queen's eyes filled with tears as she answered, "You shall have your wish, my son. The promise given both to you and to my father must be fulfilled. For, when you were but a little babe, Autolycus came to Ithaca. And one evening, as he feasted at your father's table, your nurse, Dame Eurycleia, brought you into the hall, and put you into his arms. 'Give this dear babe, O king, a name,' said she. 'He is thy daughter's son, the heir to Ithaca's rich realm; and we hope that he will live to make his name and thine remembered.'

"Then Autolycus smiled, and gently dandled you upon his knees. 'My daughter, and my daughter's lord,' said he, 'let this child's name be Odysseus; for he shall visit many lands and climes, and wander long upon the tossing sea. Yet wheresoever the Fates may drive him, his heart will ever turn to Ithaca his home. Call him by the name which I have given; and when his twelfth birthday shall have passed, send him to my strong halls in the shadow of Parnassus, where his mother in her girlhood dwelt. Then I will share my riches with him, and send him back to Ithaca rejoicing!' So spake my father, great Autolycus; and before we arose from that feast, we pledged our word that it should be with you even as he wished. And your name,

Odysseus, has every day recalled to mind that feast and our binding words."

"Oh that I could go at once, dear mother!" said Odysseus, kissing her tears away. "I would come home again very soon. I would stay long enough to have the blessing of my kingly grandfather; I would climb Parnassus, and listen to the sweet music of the Muses; I would drink one draught from the Castalian spring of which you have so often told me; I would ramble one day among the groves and glens, that perchance I might catch a glimpse of Apollo or of his huntress sister Artemis; and then I would hasten back to Ithaca, and would never leave you again."

"My son," then said Laertes, who had come unheard into the hall, and had listened to the boy's earnest words,—"my son, you shall have your wish, for I know that the Fates have ordered it so. We have long looked forward to this day, and for weeks past we have been planning for your journey. My stanchest ship is ready to carry you over the sea, and needs only to be launched into the bay. Twelve strong oarsmen are sitting now upon the beach, waiting for orders to embark. To-morrow with the bard Phemius as your friend and guide, you may set forth on your voyage to Parnassus. Let us go down to the shore at once, and offer prayers to Poseidon, ruler of the sea, that he may grant you favoring winds and a happy voyage."

Odysseus kissed his mother again, and, turning, followed his father from the hall.

Then Anticleia rose, and bade the maidens hasten to make ready the evening meal; but she herself went weeping to her own chamber, there to choose the garments which her son should take with him upon his journey. Warm robes of wool, and a broidered tunic which she with her own hands had spun and woven, she folded and laid with care in a little wooden chest; and with them she placed many a little comfort, fruit and sweetmeats, such as she rightly deemed would please the lad. Then when she had closed the lid, she threw a strong cord around the chest, and tied it firmly down. This done, she raised her eyes towards heaven, and lifting up her hands, she prayed to Pallas Athené:—

"O queen of the air and sky, hearken to my prayer, and help me lay aside the doubting fears which creep into my mind, and cause these tears to flow. For now my boy, unused to hardships, and knowing nothing of the world, is to be sent forth on a long and dangerous voyage. I tremble lest evil overtake him; but more I fear, that, with the lawless men of my father's household, he shall forget his mother's teachings, and stray from the path of duty. Do thou, O queen, go with him as his guide and guard, keep him from harm, and bring him safe again to Ithaca and his loving mother's arms."

Meanwhile Laertes and the men of Ithaca stood upon the beach, and offered up two choice oxen to Poseidon, ruler of the sea; and they prayed him that he would vouchsafe favoring winds and quiet waters and a safe journey to the bold voyagers who to-morrow would launch their ship upon the deep. And when the sun began to sink low down in the west, some sought their homes, and others went up to the king's white palace to tarry until after the evening meal.

Cheerful was the feast; and as the merry jest went round, no one seemed more free from care than King Laertes. And when all had eaten of the food, and had tasted of the red wine made from the king's own vintage, the bard Phemius arose, and tuned his harp, and sang many sweet and wonderful songs. He sang of the beginning of things; of the broad-breasted Earth, the mother of created beings; of the sky, and the sea, and the mountains; of the mighty race of Titans,—giants who once ruled the earth; of great Atlas, who holds the sky-dome upon his shoulders; of Cronos and old Oceanus; of the war which for ten years raged on Mount Olympus, until Zeus hurled his unfeeling father Cronos from the throne, and seized the sceptre for himself.

When Phemius ended his singing, the guests withdrew from the hall, and each went silently to his own home; and Odysseus, having kissed his dear father and mother, went thoughtfully to his sleeping-room high up above the great hall. With him went his nurse, Dame Eurycleia, carrying the torches. She had been a princess once; but hard fate and cruel war had overthrown her father's kingdom, and had sent her forth a captive and a slave. Laertes had bought her of her captors for a hundred oxen, and had given her a place of honor in his household next to Anticleia. She loved Odysseus as she would love her own dear child; for, since his birth, she had nursed and cared for him. She now, as was her wont, lighted him to his chamber; she laid back the soft coverings of his bed; she smoothed the fleeces, and hung his tunic within easy reach. Then with kind words of farewell for the night, she quietly withdrew, and closed the door, and pulled the thong outside which turned the fastening latch. Odysseus wrapped himself among the fleeces of his bed, and soon was lost in slumber.

ADVENTURE II

A VOYAGE ON THE SEA

EARLY the next morning, while yet the dawn was waiting for the sun, Odysseus arose and hastened to make ready for his journey. The little galley which was to carry him across the sea had been already launched, and was floating close to the shore; and the oarsmen stood upon the beach impatient to begin the voyage. The sea-stores, and the little chest in which the lad's wardrobe lay, were brought on board and placed beneath the rowers' benches. The old men of Ithaca, and the boys and the maidens, hurried down to the shore, that they might bid the voyagers God-speed. Odysseus, when all was ready, spoke a few last kind words to his mother and sage Laertes, and then with a swelling heart went up the vessel's side, and sat down in the stern. And Phemius the bard, holding his sweet-toned harp, followed him, and took his place in the prow. Then the sailors loosed the moorings, and went on board, and, sitting on the rowers' benches, wielded the long oars; and the little vessel, driven by their well-timed strokes, turned slowly about, and then glided smoothly across the bay; and the eyes of all on shore were wet with tears as they prayed the rulers of the air and the sea that the voyagers might reach their wished-for port in safety, and in due time come back unharmed to Ithaca.

No sooner had the vessel reached the open sea, than Pallas Athené sent after it a gentle west wind to urge it on its way. As the soft breeze, laden with the perfumes of blossoming orchards, stirred the water into rippling waves, Phemius bade the rowers lay aside their oars, and hoist the sail. They heeded his behest, and lifting high the slender mast, they bound it in its place; then they stretched aloft the broad white sail, and the west wind caught and filled it, and drove the little bark cheerily over the waves. And the grateful crew sat down upon the benches, and with Odysseus and Phemius the bard, they joined in offering heartfelt thanks to Pallas Athené, who had so kindly prospered them. And by and by Phemius played soft melodies on his harp, such as the sea-nymphs liked to hear. And all that summer day the breezes whispered in the rigging, and the white waves danced in the vessel's wake, and the voyagers sped happily on their way.

In the afternoon, when they had begun somewhat to tire of the voyage, Phemius asked Odysseus what they should do to lighten the passing hours.

"Tell us some story of the olden time," said Odysseus. And the bard, who was never better pleased than when recounting some wonderful tale, sat down in the midships, where the oarsmen could readily hear him, and told the strange story of Phaethon, the rash son of Helios Hyperion.

"Among the immortals who give good gifts to men, there is no one more kind than Helios, the bestower of light and heat. Every morning when the Dawn with her rosy fingers illumes the eastern sky, good Helios rises from his golden couch, and from their pasture calls his milk-white steeds. By name he calls them,—

" 'Eos, Æthon, Bronté, Astrape!'

"Each hears his master's voice, and comes obedient. Then about their bright manes and his own yellow locks he twines wreaths of sweet-smelling flowers,—amaranths and daffodils and asphodels from the heavenly gardens. And the Hours come and harness the steeds to the burning sun-car, and put the reins into Helios Hyperion's hands. He mounts to his place, he speaks,—and the winged team soars upward into the morning air; and all earth's children awake, and give thanks to the ruler of the Sun for the new day which smiles down upon them.

"Hour after hour, with steady hand, Helios guides his steeds; and the flaming car is borne along the sun-road through the sky. And when the day's work is done, and sable night comes creeping over the earth, the steeds, the car, and the driver sink softly down to the western Ocean's stream, where a golden vessel waits to bear them back again, swiftly and unseen, to the dwelling of the Sun in the east. There, under the home-roof, Helios greets his mother and his wife and his dear children; and there he rests until the Dawn again leaves old Ocean's bed, and blushing comes to bid him journey forth anew.

"One son had Helios, Phaethon the Gleaming, and among the children of men there was no one more fair. And the great heart of Helios beat with love for his earth-child, and he gave him rich gifts, and kept nothing from him.

"And Phaethon, as he grew up, became as proud as he was fair, and wherever he went he boasted of his kinship to the Sun; and men when they looked upon his matchless form and his radiant features believed his words, and honored him as the heir of Helios Hyperion. But one Epaphos, a son of Zeus, sneered.

" 'Thou a child of Helios!' he said; 'what folly! Thou canst show nothing wherewith to prove thy kinship, save thy fair face and thy yellow hair; and there are many maidens in Hellas who have those, and are as beautiful as thou. Manly grace and handsome features are indeed the gifts of the gods; but it is by godlike deeds alone that one can prove his kinship to the immortals. While Helios Hyperion—thy father, as thou wouldst have it—guides his chariot above the clouds, and showers blessings upon the earth, what dost thou do? What, indeed, but dally with thy yellow locks, and gaze upon thy costly clothing, while all the time thy feet are in the dust, and the mire of the earth holds them fast? If thou hast kinship with the gods, prove it by doing the deeds of the gods! If thou art Helios Hyperion's son, guide for one day his chariot through the skies.'

"Thus spoke Epaphos. And the mind of Phaethon was filled with lofty dreams; and, turning away from the taunting tempter, he hastened to his father's house.

"Never-tiring Helios, with his steeds and car, had just finished the course of another day; and with words of warmest love he greeted his earth-born son.

" 'Dear Phaethon,' he said, 'what errand brings thee hither at this hour, when the sons of men find rest in slumber? Is there any good gift that thou wouldst have? Say what it is, and it shall be thine.'

"And Phaethon wept. And he said, 'Father, there are those who say that I am not thy son. Give me, I pray thee, a token whereby I can prove my kinship to thee.'

"And Helios answered, 'Mine it is to labor every day, and short is the rest I have, that so earth's children may have light and life. Yet tell me what token thou cravest, and I swear that I will give it thee.'

" 'Father Helios,' said the youth, 'this is the token that I ask: Let me sit in thy place to-morrow, and drive thy steeds along the pathway of the skies.'

"Then was the heart of Helios full sad, and he said to Phaethon, 'My child, thou knowest not what

18

thou askest. Thou art not like the gods; and there lives no man who can drive my steeds, or guide the sun-car through the skies. I pray thee ask some other boon.'

"But Phaethon would not.

" 'I will have this boon or none. I will drive thy steeds to-morrow, and thereby make proof of my birthright.'

"Then Helios pleaded long with his son that he would not aspire to deeds too great for weak man to undertake. But wayward Phaethon would not hear. And when the Dawn peeped forth, and the Hours harnessed the steeds to the car, his father sadly gave the reins into his hands.

" 'My love for thee cries out, "Refrain, refrain!" Yet for my oath's sake, I grant thy wish.'

"And he hid his face, and wept.

"And Phaethon leaped into the car, and lashed the steeds with his whip. Up they sprang, and swift as a storm cloud they sped high into the blue vault of heaven. For well did they know that an unskilled hand held the reins, and proudly they scorned his control.

"The haughty heart of Phaethon sank within him, and all his courage failed; and the long reins dropped from his nerveless grasp.

" 'Glorious father,' he cried in agony, 'thy words were true. Would that I had hearkened to thy warning, and obeyed!'

"And the sun-steeds, mad with their new-gained freedom, wildly careered in mid-heaven, and then plunged downward towards the earth. Close to the peopled plains they dashed and soared, dragging the car behind them. The parched earth smoked; the rivers turned to vaporous clouds; the trees shook off their scorched leaves and died; and men and beasts hid in the caves and rocky clefts, and there perished with thirst and the unbearable heat.

" 'O Father Zeus!' prayed Mother Earth, 'send help to thy children, or they perish through this man's presumptuous folly!'

"Then the Thunderer from his high seat hurled his dread bolts, and unhappy Phaethon fell headlong from the car; and the fire-breathing steeds, affrighted but obedient, hastened back to the pastures of Helios on the shores of old Ocean's stream.

"Phaethon fell into the river which men call Eridanos, and his broken-hearted sisters wept for him; and as they stood upon the banks and bewailed his unhappy fate, Father Zeus in pity changed them into tall green poplars; and their tears, falling into the river, were hardened into precious yellow amber. But the daughters of Hesperus, through whose country this river flows, built for the fair hero a marble tomb, close by the sounding sea. And they sang a song about Phaethon, and said that although he had been hurled to the earth by the thunderbolts of angry Zeus, yet he died not without honor, for he had his heart set on the doing of great deeds."

As Phemius ended his story, Odysseus, who had been too intent upon listening to look around him, raised his eyes and uttered a cry of joy; for he saw that they had left the open sea behind them, and were entering the long and narrow gulf between Achaia and the Ætolian land. The oarsmen, who, too, had been earnest listeners, sprang quickly to their places, and hastened to ply their long oars; for now the breeze had begun to slacken, and the sail hung limp and useless upon the ship's mast. Keeping close to the northern shore they rounded capes and headlands, and skirted the mouths of deep inlets, where Phemius said strange monsters often lurked in wait for unwary or belated seafarers. But they passed all these places safely, and saw no living creature, save some flocks of sea-birds flying among the cliffs, and one lone, frightened fisherman who left his net upon the sands, and ran to hide himself in the thickets of underbrush which skirted the beach.

Late in the day they came to the mouth of a little harbor which, like one in Ithaca, was a favored haunt of old Phorcys the elder of the sea. Here the captain of the oarsmen said they must tarry for the night for the sun was already sinking in the west, and after nightfall no ship could be guided with safety along these shores. A narrow strait between high cliffs led into the little haven, which was so sheltered from the winds that vessels could ride there without their hawsers, even though fierce storms might rage upon the sea outside. Through this strait the ship was guided, urged by the strong arms of the rowers; and so swiftly did it glide across the harbor that it was driven upon the shelving beach at the farther side, and stopped not until it lay full half its length high upon the warm, dry sand.

Then the crew lifted out their store of food, and their vessels for cooking; and while some took their bows and went in search of game, others kindled a fire, and hastened to make ready the evening meal. Odysseus and his tutor, when they had climbed out of the ship, sauntered along the beach, intent to know what kind of place it was to which fortune had thus brought them. They found that it was in all things a pattern and counterpart of the little bay of Phorcys in their own Ithaca.

Near the head of the harbor grew an olive tree, beneath whose spreading branches there was a cave, in which, men said, the Naiads sometimes dwelt. In this cave were great bowls and jars and two-eared pitchers, all of stone; and in the clefts of the rock the wild bees had built their comb, and filled it with yellow honey. In this cave, too, were long looms on which, from their spindles wrought of stone, the Naiads were thought to weave their purple robes. Close by the looms, a torrent of sweet water gushed from the rock, and flowed in crystal streams down into the bay. Two doorways opened into the cave; one from the north, through which mortal man might enter, and one from the south, kept as the pathway of Phorcys and the Naiads. But Odysseus and his tutor saw no signs of any of these beings: it seemed as if the place had not been visited for many a month.

After the voyagers had partaken of their meal, they sat for a long time around the blazing fire upon the beach, and each told some marvellous story of the sea. For their thoughts were all upon the wonders of the deep.

"We should not speak of Poseidon, the king of waters," said the captain, "save with fear upon our lips, and reverence in our hearts. For he it is who rules the sea, as his brother Zeus controls the land; and no one dares to dispute his right. Once, when sailing on the Ægæan Sea, I looked down into the depths, and saw his lordly palace,—a glittering, golden mansion, built on the rocks at the bottom of the mere. Quickly did we spread our sails aloft, and the friendly breezes and our own strong arms hurried us safely away from that wonderful but dangerous station. In that palace of the deep, Poseidon eats and drinks and makes merry with his friends, the dwellers in the sea; and there he feeds and trains his swift horses,—horses with hoofs of bronze and flowing golden manes. And when he harnesses these steeds to his chariot, and wields above them his well-wrought lash of gold, you should see, as I have seen, how he rides in terrible majesty above the waves. And the creatures of the sea pilot him on his way, and gambol on either side of the car, and follow dancing in his wake. But when he smites the waters with the trident which he always carries in his hand, the waves roll mountain high, the lightnings flash, and the thunders peal, and the earth is shaken to its very core. Then it is that man bewails his own weakness, and prays to the powers above for help and succor."

"I have never seen the palace of Poseidon," said the helmsman, speaking slowly; "but once, when sailing to far-off Crete, our ship was overtaken by a storm, and for ten days we were buffeted by winds and waves, and driven into unknown seas. After this, we vainly tried to find again our reckonings, but we knew not which way to turn our vessel's prow. Then, when the storm had ended, we saw upon a sandy islet great troops of seals and sea-calves couched upon the beach, and basking in the warm rays of the sun.

" 'Let us cast anchor, and wait here,' said our captain; 'for surely Proteus, the old man of the sea who keeps Poseidon's herds, will come erewhile to look after these sea-beasts.'

"And he was right; for at noonday the herdsman of the sea came up out of the brine, and went among his sea-calves, and counted them, and called each one by name. When he was sure that not even one was missing, he lay down among them upon the sand. Then we landed quickly from our vessel, and rushed silently upon him, and seized him with our hands. The old master of magic tried hard to escape from our clutches, and did not forget his cunning. First he took the form of a long-maned lion, fierce and terrible; but when this did not affright us, he turned into a scaly serpent; then into a leopard, spotted and beautiful; then into a wild boar, with gnashing tusks and foaming mouth. Seeing that

24

by none of these forms he could make us loosen our grasp upon him, he took the shape of running water, as if to glide through our fingers; then he became a tall tree full of leaves and blossoms; and, lastly, he became himself again. And he pleaded with us for his freedom, and promised to tell us any thing that we desired, if we would only let him go.

" 'Tell us which way we shall sail, and how far we shall go, that we may surely reach the fair harbor of Crete,' said our captain.

" 'Sail with the wind two days,' said the elder of the sea, 'and on the third morning ye shall behold the hills of Crete, and the pleasant port which you seek.'

"Then we loosened our hold upon him, and old Proteus plunged into the briny deep; and we betook ourselves to our ship, and sailed away before the wind. And on the third day, as he had told us, we sighted the fair harbor of Crete."

As the helmsman ended his story, his listeners smiled; for he had told them nothing but an old tale, which every seaman had learned in his youth,—the story of Proteus, symbol of the ever-changing forms of matter. Just then Odysseus heard a low, plaintive murmur, seeming as if uttered by some lost wanderer away out upon the sea.

"What is that?" he asked, turning towards Phemius.

"It is Glaucus, the soothsayer of the sea, lamenting that he is mortal," answered the bard.

"Long time ago, Glaucus was a poor fisherman who cast his nets into these very waters, and built his hut upon the Ætolian shore, not very far from the place where we now sit. Before his hut there was a green, grassy spot, where he often sat to dress the fish which he caught. One day he carried a basketful of half-dead fish to that spot, and turned them out upon the ground. Wonderful to behold! Each fish took a blade of grass in its mouth, and forthwith jumped into the sea. The next day he found a hare in the woods, and gave chase to it. The frightened creature ran straight to the grassy plat before his hut, seized a green spear of grass between its lips, and dashed into the sea.

" 'Strange what kind of grass that is!' cried Glaucus. Then he pulled up a blade, and tasted it. Quick as thought, he also jumped into the sea; and there he wanders evermore among the seaweeds and the sand and the pebbles and the sunken rocks; and, although he has the gift of soothsaying, and can tell what things are in store for mortal men, he mourns and laments because he cannot die."

Then Phemius, seeing that Odysseus grew tired of his story, took up his harp, and touched its strings, and sang a song about old Phorcys,—the son of the Sea and Mother Earth,—and about his strange daughters who dwell in regions far remote from the homes of men.

He touched his harp lightly, and sang a sweet lullaby,—a song about the Sirens, the fairest of all the daughters of old Phorcys. These have their home in an enchanted island in the midst of the western sea; and they sit in a green meadow by the shore, and they sing evermore of empty pleasures and of phantoms of delight and of vain expectations. And woe is the wayfaring man who hearkens to them! for by their bewitching tones they lure him to his death, and never again shall he see his dear wife or his babes, who wait long and vainly for his home-coming. Stop thine ears, O voyager on the sea, and listen not to the songs of the Sirens, sing they ever so sweetly; for the white flowers which dot the meadow around them are not daisies, but the bleached bones of their victims.

Then Phemius smote the chords of his harp, and played a melody so weird and wild that Odysseus sprang to his feet, and glanced quickly around him, as if he thought to see some grim and horrid shape threatening him from among the gathering shadows. And this time the bard sang a strange, tumultuous song, concerning other daughters of old Phorcys,—the three Gray Sisters, with shape of swan, who have but one tooth for all, and one common eye, and who sit forever on a barren rock near the farthest shore of Ocean's stream. Upon them the sun doth never cast a beam, and the moon doth never look; but, horrible and alone, they sit clothed in their yellow robes, and chatter threats and meaningless complaints to the waves which dash against their rock.

Not far away from these monsters once sat the three Gorgons, daughters also of old Phorcys.

These were clothed with bat-like wings, and horror sat upon their faces. They had ringlets of snakes for hair, and their teeth were like the tusks of swine, and their hands were talons of brass; and no mortal could ever gaze upon them and breathe again. But there came, one time, a young hero to those regions,—Perseus the godlike; and he snatched the eye of the three Gray Sisters, and flung it far into the depths of Lake Tritonis; and he slew Medusa, the most fearful of the Gorgons, and carried the head of the terror back to Hellas with him as a trophy.

The bard chose next a gentler theme: and, as he touched his harp, the listeners fancied that they heard the soft sighing of the south wind, stirring lazily the leaves and blossoms; they heard the plashing of fountains, and the rippling of water-brooks, and the songs of little birds; and their minds were carried away in memory to pleasant gardens in a summer land. And Phemius sang of the Hesperides, or the maidens of the West, who also, men say, are the daughters of Phorcys the ancient. The Hesperian land in which they dwell is a country of delight, where the trees are laden with golden fruit, and every day is a sweet dream of joy and peace. And the clear-voiced Hesperides sing and dance in the sunlight always; and their only task is to guard the golden apples which grow there, and which Mother Earth gave to Here the queen upon her wedding day.

Here Phemius paused. Odysseus, lulled by the soft music, and overcome by weariness, had lain down upon the sand and fallen asleep. At a sign from the bard, the seamen lifted him gently into the ship, and, covering him with warm skins, they left him to slumber through the night.

ADVENTURE III

THE CENTRE OF THE EARTH

THE next morning, before the sun had risen, the voyagers launched their ship again, and sailed out of the little harbor into the long bay of Crissa. And Pallas Athené sent the west wind early, to help them forward on their way; and they spread their sail, and instead of longer hugging the shore, they ventured boldly out into the middle of the bay. All day long the ship held on its course, skimming swiftly through the waves like a great white-winged bird; and those on board beguiled the hours with song and story as on the day before. But when the evening came, they were far from land; and the captain said that as the water was deep, and he knew the sea quite well, they would not put into port, but would sail straight on all night. And so, when the sun had gone down, and the moon had risen, flooding earth and sea with her pure, soft light, Odysseus wrapped his warm cloak about him, and lay down again to rest upon his bed of skins between the rowers' benches. But the helmsman stood at his place, and guided the vessel over the shadowy waves; and through the watches of the night, the west wind filled the sails, and the dark keel of the little bark ploughed the waters, and Pallas Athené blessed the voyage.

When, at length, the third morning came, and Helios arose at summons of the Dawn, Odysseus awoke. To his great surprise, he heard no longer the rippling of the waves upon the vessel's sides, nor the flapping of the sail in the wind, nor yet the rhythmic dipping of the oars into the sea. He listened, and the sound of merry laughter came to his ears, and he heard the twittering of many birds, and the far-away bleating of little lambs. He rubbed his eyes, and sat up, and looked about him. The ship was no longer floating on the water, but had been drawn high up on a sandy beach; and the crew were sitting beneath an olive tree, at no great distance from the shore, listening to the melodies with which a strangely-garbed shepherd welcomed on his flute the coming of another day.

Odysseus arose quickly and leaped out upon the beach. Then it was that a scene of beauty and quiet grandeur met his gaze,—a scene, the like of which had never entered his thoughts nor visited his dreams. He saw, a few miles to the northward, a group of high mountains whose summits towered above the clouds; and highest among them all were twin peaks whose snow-crowned tops seemed but little lower than the skies themselves. And as the light of the newly risen sun gilded the gray crags, and painted the rocky slopes, and shone bright among the wooded uplands, the whole scene appeared like a living picture, glorious with purple and gold and azure, and brilliant with sparkling gems.

"Is it not truly a fitting place for the home of beauty and music, the dwelling of Apollo, and the favored haunt of the Muses?" asked Phemius, drawing near, and observing the boy's wondering delight.

"Indeed it is," said Odysseus, afraid to turn his eyes away, lest the enchanting vision should vanish like a dream. "But is that mountain really Parnassus, and is our journey so nearly at an end?"

"Yes," answered the bard, "that peak which towers highest toward the sky is great Parnassus, the centre of the earth; and in the rocky cleft which you can barely see between the twin mountains, stands sacred Delphi and the favored temple of Apollo. Lower down, and on the other side of the mountain, is the white-halled dwelling of old Autolycus, your mother's father. Although the mountain seems so near, it is yet a long and toilsome journey thither,—a journey which we must make on foot, and by pathways none the safest. Come, let us join the sailors under the olive tree; and when we have breakfasted, we will begin our journey to Parnassus."

The strange shepherd had killed the fattest sheep of his flock, and had roasted the choicest parts upon a bed of burning coals; and when Odysseus and his tutor came to the olive tree, they found a breakfast fit indeed for kings, set out ready before them.

"Welcome, noble strangers," said the shepherd; "welcome to the land most loved of the Muses. I give you of the best of all that I have, and I am ready to serve you and do your bidding."

Phemius thanked the shepherd for his kindness; and while they sat upon the grass, and ate of the pleasant food which had been provided, he asked the simple swain many questions about Parnassus.

"I have heard that Parnassus is the hub around which the great earth-wheel is built. Is it really true?"

"A long, long time ago," answered the man, "there were neither any shepherds nor sheep in Hellas, and not even the gods knew where the centre of the earth had been put. Some said that it was at Mount Olympus, where Zeus sits in his great house with all the deathless ones around him. Others said that it was in Achaia; and others still, in Arcadia, now the land of shepherds; and some, who, it seems to me, had lost their wits, said that it was not in Hellas at all, but in a strange land beyond the western sea. In order that he might know the truth, great Zeus one day took two eagles, both of the same strength and swiftness, and said, 'These birds shall tell us what even the gods do not know.' Then he carried one of the eagles to the far east, where the Dawn rises out of Ocean's bed; and he carried the other to the far west where Helios and his sun-car sink into the waves; and he clapped his hands together, and the thunder rolled, and the swift birds flew at the same moment to meet each other; and right above the spot where Delphi stands, they came together, beak to beak, and both fell dead to the ground. 'Behold! there is the centre of the earth,' said Zeus. And all the gods agreed that he was right."

"Do you know the best and shortest road to Delphi?" asked Phemius.

"No one knows it better than I," was the answer. "When I was a boy I fed my sheep at the foot of Parnassus; and my father and grandfather lived there, long before the town of Delphi was built, or there was any temple there for Apollo. Shall I tell you how men came to build a temple at that spot?"

"Yes, tell us," said Odysseus. "I am anxious to know all about it."

"You must not repeat my story to the priests at Delphi," said the shepherd, speaking now in a lower tone. "For they have quite a different way of telling it, and they would say that I have spoken lightly of sacred things. There was a time when only shepherds lived on the mountain slopes, and there were neither priests nor warriors nor robbers in all this land. My grandfather was one of those happy shepherds; and he often pastured his flocks on the broad terrace where the town of Delphi now stands, and where the two eagles, which I have told you about, fell to the ground. One day, a strange thing happened to him. A goat which was nibbling the grass from the sides of a little crevice in the rock, fell into a fit, and lay bleating and helpless upon the ground. My grandfather ran to help the beast; but as he stooped down, he too fell into a fit, and he saw strange visions, and spoke prophetic words. Some other shepherds who were passing by saw his plight, and lifted him up; and as soon as he breathed the fresh air, he was himself again.

"Often after this, the same thing happened to my grandfather's goats; and when he had looked carefully into the matter, he found that a warm, stifling vapor issued at times from the crevice, and that it was the breathing of this vapor which had caused his goats and even himself to lose their senses. Then other men came; and they learned that by sitting close to the crevice, and inhaling its vapor, they gained the power to foresee things, and the gift of prophecy came to them. And so they set a tripod over the crevice for a seat, and they built a temple—small at first—over the tripod; and they sent for the wisest maidens in the land to come and sit upon the tripod, and breathe the strange vapor, so that they could tell what was otherwise hidden from human knowledge. Some say that the vapor is the breath of a python, or great serpent; and they call the priestess who sits upon the tripod Pythia. But I know nothing about that."

"Are you sure," asked Phemius, "that it was your grandfather who first found that crevice in the rock?"

"I am not quite sure," said the shepherd. "But I heard the story when I was a little child, and I know that it was either my grandfather or my grand-father's grandfather. At any rate, it all happened many, many years ago."

By this time they had finished their meal; and after they had given thanks to the powers who had thus far kindly prospered them, they hastened to renew their journey. Two of the oarsmen, who were landsmen as well as seamen, were to go with them to carry their luggage and the little presents which Laertes had sent to the priests at Delphi. The shepherd was to be their guide; and a second shepherd was to keep them company, so as to help them in case of need.

The sun was high over their heads when they were ready to begin their long and toilsome walk. The road at first was smooth and easy, winding through meadows and orchards and shady pastures. But very soon the way became steep and uneven, and the olive trees gave place to pines, and the meadows to barren rocks. The little company toiled bravely onward, however, the two shepherds leading the way and cheering them with pleasant melodies on their flutes, while the two sailors with their heavy loads followed in the rear.

It was quite late in the day when they reached the sacred town of Delphi, nestling in the very bosom of Parnassus. The mighty mountain wall now rose straight up before them, seeming to reach even to the clouds. The priests who kept the temple met them on the outskirts of the town, and kindly welcomed them for the sake of King Laertes, whom they knew and had seen; and they besought the wayfarers to abide for some time in Delphi. Nor, indeed, would Phemius have thought of going farther until he had prayed to bright Apollo, and offered rich gifts at his shrine, and questioned the Pythian priestess about the unknown future.

And so Odysseus and his tutor became the honored guests of the Delphian folk; and they felt that surely they were now at the very centre of the world. Their hosts dealt so kindly with them, that a whole month passed, and still they were in Delphi. And as they talked with the priests in the temple, or listened to the music of the mountain nymphs, or drank sweet draughts of wisdom from the Castalian spring, they every day found it harder and harder to tear themselves away from the delightful place.

THE SILVER-BOWED APOLLO

ONE morning Odysseus sat in the shadow of Parnassus with one of the priests of Apollo, and they talked of many wonderful things; and the boy began to think to himself that there was more wisdom in the words of his companion than in all the waters of the Castalian spring. He could see, from where he sat, the stream of that far-famed fountain, flowing out of the rocks between two cliffs, and falling in sparkling cascades down the steep slopes.

"Men think that they gain wisdom by drinking from that spring," said he to the priest; "but I think that they gain it in quite another way. They drink of its waters every day; but while they drink, they listen to the wonderful words which fall from your lips, and they become wise by hearing, and not by drinking."

The old priest smiled at the shrewdness of the boy. "Let them think as they please," said he. "In any case, their wisdom would come hard, and be of little use, if it were not for the silver-bowed Apollo."

"Tell me about Apollo," said Odysseus.

The priest could not have been better pleased. He moved his seat, so that he could look the boy full in the face, and at the same time have the temple before him, and then he began:—

"A very long time ago, Apollo was born in distant Delos. And when the glad news of his birth was told, Earth smiled, and decked herself with flowers; the nymphs of Delos sang songs of joy that were heard to the utmost bounds of Hellas; and choirs of white swans flew seven times around the island, piping notes of praise to the pure being who had come to dwell among men. Then Zeus looked down from high Olympus, and crowned the babe with a golden head-band, and put into his hands a silver bow and a sweet-toned lyre such as no man had ever seen; and he gave him a team of white swans to drive, and bade him go forth to teach men the things which are right and good, and to make light that which is hidden and in darkness.

"And so Apollo arose, beautiful as the morning sun, and journeyed through many lands, seeking a dwelling-place. He stopped for a time at the foot of Mount Olympus, and played so sweetly upon his lyre that Zeus and all his court were entranced. Then he went into Pieria and Iolcos, and he wandered up and down through the whole length of the Thessalian land; but nowhere could he find a spot in which he was willing to dwell. Then he climbed into his car, and bade his swan-team fly with

him to the country of the Hyperboreans beyond the
far-off northern mountains. Forthwith they obeyed;
and through the pure regions of the upper air they
bore him, winging their way ever northward. They
carried him over the desert flats where the shepherd
folk of Scythia dwell in houses of wicker-work
perched on well-wheeled wagons, and daily drive
their flocks and herds to fresher pastures. They
carried him over that unknown land where the
Arimaspian host of one-eyed horsemen dwell beside
a river running bright with gold; and on the seventh
day they came to the great Rhipæan Mountains
where the griffins, with lion bodies and eagle wings,
guard the golden treasures of the North. In these
mountains, the North Wind has his home; and from
his deep caves he now and then comes forth, chilling
with his cold and angry breath the orchards and the
fair fields of Hellas, and bringing death and dire
disasters in his train. But northward this blustering
Boreas cannot blow, for the heaven-towering
mountains stand like a wall against him, and drive
him back; and hence it is that beyond these
mountains the storms of winter never come, but one
happy springtime runs through all the year. There
the flowers bloom, and the grain ripens, and the
fruits drop mellowing to the earth, and the red wine
is pressed from the luscious grape, every day the
same. And the Hyperboreans who dwell in that
favored land know neither pain nor sickness, nor
wearying labor nor eating care; but their youth is as
unfading as the springtime, and old age with its
wrinkles and its sorrows is evermore a stranger to

them. For the spirit of evil, which leads all men to err, has never found entrance among them, and they are free from vile passions and unworthy thoughts; and among them there is neither war, nor wicked deeds, nor fear of the avenging Furies, for their hearts are pure and clean, and never burdened with the love of self.

"When the swan-team of silver-bowed Apollo had carried him over the Rhipæan Mountains, they alighted in the Hyperborean land. And the people welcomed Apollo with shouts of joy and songs of triumph, as one for whom they had long been waiting. And he took up his abode there, and dwelt with them one whole year, delighting them with his presence, and ruling over them as their king. But when twelve moons had passed, he bethought him that the toiling, suffering men of Hellas needed most his aid and care. Therefore he bade the Hyperboreans farewell, and again went up into his sun-bright car; and his winged team carried him back to the land of his birth.

"Long time Apollo sought a place where he might build a temple to which men might come to learn of him and to seek his help in time of need. At length he came to the plain of fair Tilphussa, by the shore of Lake Copais; and there he began to build a house, for the land was a pleasant one, well-watered, and rich in grain and fruit. But the nymph Tilphussa liked not to have Apollo dwell so near her, lest men seeing and loving him should forget to honor her; and one day, garmented with mosses and crowned with lilies, she came and stood before him in the sunlight.

" 'Apollo of the silver bow,' said she, 'have you not made a mistake in choosing this place for a dwelling? These rich plains around us will not always be as peaceful as now; for their very richness will tempt the spoiler, and the song of the cicada will then give place to the din of battle. Even in times of peace, you would hardly have a quiet hour here: for great herds of cattle come crowding down every day to my lake for water; and the noisy ploughman, driving his team afield, disturbs the morning hour with his boorish shouts; and boys and dogs keep up a constant din, and make life in this place a burden.'

" 'Fair Tilphussa,' said Apollo, 'I had hoped to dwell here in thy happy vale, a neighbor and friend to thee. Yet, since this place is not what it seems to be, whither shall I go, and where shall I build my house?'

" 'Go to the cleft in Parnassus where the swift eagles of Zeus met above the earth's centre,' answered the nymph. 'There thou canst dwell in peace, and men will come from all parts of the world to do thee honor.'

"And so Apollo came down towards Crissa, and here in the cleft of the mountain he laid the foundations of his shrine. Then he called the master-architects of the world, Trophonius and Agamedes, and gave to them the building of the high walls and the massive roof. And when they had finished their work, he said, 'Say now what reward you most desire for your labor, and I will give it you.'

" 'Give us,' said the brothers, 'that which is the best for men.'

" 'It is well,' answered Apollo. 'When the full moon is seen above the mountain-tops, you shall have your wish.'

"But when the moon rose full and clear above the heights, the two brothers were dead.

"And Apollo was pleased with the place which he had chosen for a home; for here were peace and quiet, and neither the hum of labor nor the din of battle would be likely ever to enter. Yet there was one thing to be done before he could have perfect rest. There lived near the foot of the mountain a huge serpent called Python, which was the terror of all the land. Oftentimes, coming out of his den, this monster attacked the flocks and herds, and sometimes even their keepers; and he had been known to carry little children and helpless women to his den, and there devour them.

"The men of Delphi came one day to Apollo, and prayed him to drive out or destroy their terrible enemy. So, taking in hand his silver bow, he sallied out at break of day to meet the monster when he should issue from his slimy cave. The vile creature shrank back when he saw the radiant god before him, and would fain have hidden himself in the deep gorges of the mountain. But Apollo quickly launched a swift arrow at him, crying, 'Thou bane of man, lie thou upon the earth, and enrich it with thy dead body!' And the never-erring arrow sped to the mark; and the great beast died, wallowing in his gore. And the people in their joy came out to meet the archer, singing pæans in his praise; and they crowned him with wild flowers and wreaths of olives, and hailed him as the Pythian king; and the nightingales sang to him in the groves, and the swallows and cicadas twittered and tuned their melodies in harmony with his lyre.

"But as yet there were no priests in Apollo's temple; and he pondered, long doubting, as to whom he should choose. One day he stood upon the mountain's topmost peak, whence he could see all Hellas and the seas around it. Far away in the south, he spied a little ship sailing from Crete to sandy Pylos; and the men who were on board were Cretan merchants.

" 'These men shall serve in my temple!' he cried.

"Upward he sprang, and high he soared above the sea; then swiftly descending like a fiery star, he plunged into the waves. There he changed himself into the form of a dolphin, and swam with speed to overtake the vessel. Long before the ship had reached Pylos, the mighty fish came up with it, and struck its stern. The crew were dumb with terror, and sat still in their places; their oars were motionless; the sail hung limp and useless from the mast. Yet the vessel sped through the waves with the speed of the wind, for the dolphin was driving it forward by the force of his fins. Past many a headland, past Pylos and many pleasant harbors, they hastened. Vainly did the pilot try to land at Cyparissa and at Cyllene: the ship would not obey her helm. They rounded the headland of Araxus, and came into the long bay of Crissa; and there the dolphin left off guiding the vessel, and swam playfully around it, while a brisk west wind filled the sail, and bore the voyagers safely into port.

"Then the dolphin changed into the form of a glowing star, which, shooting high into the heavens, lit up the whole world with its glory; and as the awe-stricken crew stood gazing at the wonder, it fell with the quickness of light upon Parnassus. Into his temple Apollo hastened, and there he kindled an undying fire. Then, in the form of a handsome youth, with golden hair falling in waves upon his shoulders, he hastened to the beach to welcome the Cretan strangers.

" 'Hail, seamen!' he cried. 'Who are you, and from whence do you come? Shall I greet you as friends and guests, or shall I know you as robbers bringing death and distress to many a fair home?'

"Then answered the Cretan captain, 'Fair stranger, the gods have brought us hither; for by no wish of our own have we come. We are Cretan merchants, and we were on our way to sandy Pylos with stores of merchandise, to barter with the tradesmen of that city. But some unknown being, whose might is greater than the might of men, has carried us far beyond our wished-for port, even to this unknown shore. Tell us now, we pray thee, what land is this? And who art thou who lookest so like a god?'

" 'Friends and guests, for such indeed you must be,' answered the radiant youth, 'think never again of sailing upon the wine-faced sea, but draw now your vessel high up on the beach. And when you have brought out all your goods, and built an altar upon the shore, take of your white barley which you have with you, and offer it reverently to Phœbus Apollo. For I am he; and it was I who brought you hither, so that you might keep my temple, and make known my wishes unto men. And since it was in the form of a dolphin that you first saw me, let the town which stands around my temple be known as Delphi, and let men worship me there as Apollo Delphinius.'

"Then the Cretans did as he had bidden them: they drew their vessel high up on the white beach, and when they had unladen it of their goods, they built an altar on the shore, and offered white barley to Phœbus Apollo, and gave thanks to the ever-living powers who had saved them from the terrors of the deep. And after they had feasted, and rested from their long voyage, they turned their faces toward Parnassus; and Apollo, playing sweeter music than men had ever heard, led the way; and the folk of Delphi, with choirs of boys and maidens, came to meet them, and they sang a pæan and songs of victory as they helped the Cretans up the steep pathway to the cleft of Parnassus.

" 'I leave you now to have sole care of my temple,' said Apollo. 'I charge you to keep it well; deal righteously with all men; let no unclean thing pass your lips; forget self; guard well your thoughts, and keep your hearts free from guile. If you do these things, you shall be blessed with length of days, and all that makes life glad. But if you forget my words, and deal treacherously with men, and cause any to wander from the path of right, then shall you be driven forth homeless and accursed, and others shall take your places in the service of my house.'

"And then the bright youth left them, and hastened away into Thessaly and to Mount Olympus. But, every year he comes again, and looks into his house, and speaks words of warning and of hope to his servants; and often men have seen him on Parnassus, playing; his lyre to the listening Muses, or with his sister, arrow-loving Artemis, chasing the mountain deer."

Such was the story which the old priest related to Odysseus, sitting in the shadow of the mountain; and the boy listened with eyes wide open and full of wonder, half expecting to see the golden-haired Apollo standing by his side.

ADVENTURE V

THE KING OF CATTLE THIEVES

ODYSSEUS and his tutor tarried, as I have told you, a whole month at Delphi; for Phemius would not venture farther on their journey until the Pythian oracle should tell him how it would end. In the mean while many strangers were daily coming from all parts of Hellas, bringing rich gifts for Apollo's temple, and seeking advice from the Pythia. From these strangers Odysseus learned many things concerning lands and places of which he never before had heard; and nothing pleased him better than to listen to the marvellous tales which each man told about his own home and people.

One day as he was walking towards the spring of Castalia, an old man, who had come from Corinth to ask questions of the Pythia, met him, and stopped to talk with him.

"Young prince," said the old man, "what business can bring one so young as you to this place sacred to Apollo?"

"I am on my way to visit my grandfather," said Odysseus, "and I have stopped here for a few days while my tutor consults the oracle."

"Your grandfather! And who is your grandfather?" asked the old man.

"The great chief Autolycus, whose halls are on the other side of Parnassus," answered Odysseus.

The old man drew a long breath, and after a moment's silence said, "Perhaps, then, you are going to help your grandfather take care of his neighbors' cattle."

"I do not know what you mean," answered Odysseus, startled by the tone in which the stranger spoke these words.

"I mean that your grandfather, who is the most cunning of men, will expect to teach you his trade," said the man, with a strange twinkle in his eye.

"My grandfather is a chieftain and a hero," said the boy. "What trade has he?"

"You pretend not to know that he is a cattle-dealer," answered the old man, shrugging his shoulders. "Why, all Hellas has known him these hundred years as the King of Cattle Thieves! But he is very old now, and the herdsmen and shepherds have little to fear from him any more. Yet, mind my words, young prince: it does not require the wisdom of the Pythian oracle to foretell that you, his grandson, will become the craftiest of men. With

Autolycus for your grandfather and Hermes for your great-grandfather, it would be hard indeed for you to be otherwise."

At this moment the bard Phemius came up, and the old man walked quickly away.

"What does he mean?" asked Odysseus, turning to his tutor. "What does he mean by saying that my grandfather is the king of cattle thieves, and by speaking of Hermes as my great-grandfather?"

"They tell strange tales about Autolycus, the mountain chief," Phemius answered; "but whether their stories be true or false, I cannot say. The old man who was talking to you is from Corinth, where once reigned Sisyphus, a most cruel and crafty king. From Corinth, Sisyphus sent ships and traders to all the world; and the wealth of Hellas might have been his, had he but loved the truth and dealt justly with his fellow-men. But there was no honor in his soul; he betrayed his dearest friends for gold; and he crushed under a huge block of stone the strangers who came to Corinth to barter their merchandise. It is said, that, once upon a time, Autolycus went down to Corinth in the night, and carried away all the cattle of Sisyphus, driving them to his great pastures beyond Parnassus. Not long afterward, Sisyphus went boldly to your grandfather's halls, and said,—

" 'I have come, Autolycus, to get again my cattle which you have been so kindly pasturing.'

" 'It is well,' said Autolycus. 'Go now among my herds, and if you find any cattle bearing your mark upon them, they are yours: drive them back to your own pastures. This is the offer which I make to every man who comes claiming that I have stolen his cattle.'

"Then Sisyphus, to your grandfather's great surprise, went among the herds, and chose his own without making a single error.

" 'See you not my initial, Σ, under the hoof of each of these beasts?' asked Sisyphus.

"Autolycus saw at once that he had been outwitted, and he fain would have made friends with one who was more crafty than himself. But Sisyphus dealt treacherously with him, as he did with every one who trusted him. Yet men say, that, now he is dead, he has his reward in Hades; for there he is doomed to the never-ending toil of heaving a heavy stone to the top of a hill, only to see it roll back again to the plain. It was from him that men learned to call your grandfather the King of Cattle Thieves; with how much justice, you may judge for yourself."

"You have explained a part of what I asked you," said Odysseus thoughtfully, "but you have not answered my question about Hermes."

"I will answer that at another time," said Phemius; "for to-morrow we must renew our journey, and I must go now and put every thing in readiness."

"But has the oracle spoken?" asked Odysseus in surprise.

51

"The Pythia has answered my question," said the bard. "I asked what fortune should attend you on this journey, and the oracle made this reply:—

'To home and kindred he shall safe return ere long,
  With scars well-won, and greeted with triumphal song.' "

"What does it mean?" asked Odysseus.

"Just what it says," answered the bard. "All that is now needed is that we should do our part, and fortune will surely smile upon us."

And so, on the morrow, they bade their kind hosts farewell, and began to climb the steep pathway, which, they were told, led up and around to the rock-built halls of Autolycus. At the top of the first slope they came upon a broad table-land from the centre of which rose the peak of Parnassus towering to the skies. Around the base of this peak, huge rocks were piled, one above the other, just as they had been thrown in the days of old from the mighty hands of the Titans. On every side were clefts and chasms and deep gorges, through which flowed roaring torrents fed from the melting snows above. And in the sides of the cliffs were dark caves and narrow grottos, hollowed from the solid rock, wherein strange creatures were said to dwell.

Now and then Odysseus fancied that he saw a mountain nymph flitting among the trees, or a satyr with shaggy beard hastily hiding himself among the clefts and crags above them. They passed by the great Corycian cavern, whose huge vaulted chambers would shelter a thousand men; but they looked in vain for the nymph Corycia, who, they were told, sometimes sat within, and smiled upon passing travellers. A little farther beyond, they heard the mellow notes of a lyre, and the sound of laughter and merry-making, in a grove of evergreens, lower down the mountain-side; and Odysseus wondered if Apollo and the Muses were not there.

The path which the little company followed did not lead to the summit of the peak, but wound around its base, and then, by many a zigzag, led downward to a wooded glen through the middle of which a mountain torrent rushed. By and by the glen widened into a pleasant valley, broad and green, bounded on three sides by steep mountain walls. Here were rich pasture-lands, and a meadow, in which Odysseus saw thousands of cattle grazing. The guide told them that those were the pastures and the cattle of great Autolycus. Close to the bank of the mountain torrent,—just where it leaped from a precipice, and, forgetting its wild hurry, was changed to a quiet meadow brook,—stood the dwelling of the chief. It was large and low and had been hewn out of the solid rock; it looked more like the entrance to a mountain cave than like the palace of a king.

Odysseus and his tutor walked boldly into the great hall; for the low doorway was open and unguarded, and the following words were roughly carved in the rock above: "Here lives Autolycus. If your heart is brave, enter." They passed through the entrance-hall, and came to a smaller inner chamber. There they saw Autolycus seated in a chair of ivory and gold, thick-cushioned with furs; and near him sat fair Amphithea his wife, busy with her spindle and distaff. The chief was very old; his white hair fell in waves upon his great shoulders, and his broad brow was wrinkled with age: yet his frame was that of a giant, and his eyes glowed and sparkled with the fire of youth.

"Strangers," said he kindly, "you are welcome to my halls. It is not often that men visit me in my mountain home, and old age has bound me here in my chair so that I can no longer walk abroad among my fellows. Besides this, there are those who of late speak many unkind words of me; and good men care not to be the guests of him who is called the King of Cattle Thieves." Then seeing that his visitors still lingered at the door, he added, "I pray you, whoever you may be, fear not, but enter, and be assured of a kind welcome."

Then Odysseus went fearlessly forward, and stood before the chief, and made himself known, and showed them the presents which his mother Anticleia had sent. Glad indeed was the heart of old Autolycus as he grasped the hand of his grandson; and Amphithea took the lad in her arms, and kissed his brow and both his eyes, and wept for very fulness of joy. Then, at a call from the old chief, an inner door was opened, and his six sons came in. Stalwart men were they, with limbs strong as iron, and eyes like those of the mountain eagle; and they warmly welcomed the young prince, and asked him a thousand questions about his home in Ithaca, and his queen-mother, their sister Anticleia.

"Waste not the hours in talk!" cried old Autolycus at last. "There is yet another day for words. Make ready at once a fitting feast for this my grandson and his friend the bard; and let our halls ring loud with joyful merriment."

The sons at once obeyed. From the herd which was pasturing in the meadows, they chose the fattest calf; this they slew and quickly dressed; and then, cutting off the choicest parts, they roasted them on spits before the blazing fire. And when the meal was ready, great Autolycus, his wife, and his sons sat down with their guests at the heavy-laden table; and they feasted merrily until the sun went down, and darkness covered the earth. Then the young men brought arm-loads of dry branches, and logs of pine, and threw them upon the fire, and the blaze leaped up and lighted the hall with a rich ruddy glow; and Odysseus sat upon a couch of bearskins, at his grandfather's feet, and listened to many a wonderful story of times long past, but ever present in the old man's memory.

"Truly there are two things against which it is useless for any man to fight," said Autolycus, "and these are old age and death. The first has already made me his slave, and the second will soon have me in his clutches. When I was young, there was not a man who could outstrip me in the foot race. I even thought myself a match for the fleet-footed maiden

Atalanta. There were very few men, even among the great heroes, who could hurl a spear with more force than I; and there was hardly one who could bend my great bow. But now both spear and bow are useless. You see them standing in the corner there, where my eyes can rest upon them. To-morrow you shall help me polish them."

Then after a moment's pause he added, "But, oh the wrestling and the leaping! There was never but one mortal who could excel me in either."

"I have heard," said Odysseus, "that even great Heracles was your pupil."

"And such indeed he was," answered the old man. "The first time I saw the matchless hero, he was but a child, tall and beautiful, with the eyes of a wild deer, and with flaxen hair falling over his shoulders. But he was stronger even then than any common mortal. His stepfather Amphitryon called me to Thebes to be the boy's teacher, for he saw in him rich promises of future greatness. With me he called many of the noblest men of Hellas. First there was Eurytus, the master of archers, who taught the hero how to bend the bow, and send the swift arrow straight to the mark. But in an evil day Eurytus met his fate, and all through his own folly. For, being proud of his skill, which no mortal could excel, he challenged great Apollo to a shooting match; and the angry archer-god pierced him through and through with his arrows.

"Second among the teachers of Heracles was Castor, the brother of Polydeuces and of Helen, the most beautiful of women. He taught the hero how to wield the spear and the sword. Then, there was Linus, the brother of Orpheus, sweetest of musicians, who came to teach him how to touch the lyre and bring forth bewitching melody; but the boy, whose mind was set on great deeds, cared naught for music, and the lessons which Linus gave him were profitless. 'Thou art but a dull and witless youth!' cried the minstrel one day, striking his pupil upon the cheek. Then Heracles in wrath smote Linus with his own lyre, and killed him. 'Even a dull pupil has his rights,' said he, 'and one of these is the right not to be called a blockhead.' The Theban rulers brought the young hero to trial for his crime; but he stood up before them, and reminded them of a half-forgotten law which Rhadamanthus, the ruler of the Elysian land, had given them: *'Whoso defends himself against an unjust attack is guiltless, and shall go free.'* And the judges, pleased with his wisdom, gave him his liberty."

"Did Heracles have any other teachers?" asked Odysseus, anxious to hear more.

"Yes; Amphitryon himself taught the lad how to drive a chariot skilfully, and how to manage horses. And, as I have said, he called me to teach him the manly arts of leaping and running and wrestling. He was an apt pupil, and soon excelled his master; and Amphitryon, fearing that in a thoughtless moment he might serve me as he had served unlucky Linus, sent him away to Mount

57

Cithæron to watch his herds which were pasturing there."

"Surely," said Odysseus, looking at the giant arms of his grandfather, ridged with iron muscles,— "surely there was no danger of the young hero harming you."

"A son of Hermes, such as I," said the old chief, "might dare to stand against Heracles in craft and cunning, but never in feats of strength. While the lad fed Amphitryon's flocks in the mountain meadows, he grew to be a giant, four cubits in height, and terrible to look upon. His voice was like the roar of a desert lion; his step was like the march of an earthquake; and fire flashed from his eyes like the glare of thunderbolts when they are hurled from the storm clouds down to the fruitful plains below. He could tear up trees by their roots, and hurl mountain crags from their places. It was then that he slew the Cithæron lion with his bare hands, and took its skin for a helmet and a mantle which, I am told, he wears to this very day. Only a little while after this, he led the Thebans into a battle with their enemies, the Minyans, and gained for them a glorious victory. Then Pallas Athené, well pleased with the hero, gave him a purple robe; Hephaestus made for him a breastplate of solid gold; and Hermes gave him a sword, Apollo a bow, and Poseidon a team of the most wonderful horses ever known. Then, that he might be fully armed, he went into the Nemæan wood, and cut for himself that stout club which he always carries, and which is more terrible in his hands than spear, or sword, or bow and arrows."

"I have heard," said Odysseus, "that Cheiron, the centaur, was one of the teachers of Heracles."

"He was not only his teacher," said Autolycus, "but he was his friend. He taught what was just and true; he showed him that there is one thing greater than strength, and that is gentleness; and he led him to change his rude, savage nature into one full of kindness and love: so that in all the world there is no one so full of pity for the poor and weak, so full of sympathy for the down-trodden, as is Heracles the strong. Had it not been for wise Cheiron, I fear that Heracles would not have made the happy decision which he once did, when the choice of two roads was offered him."

"What was that?" asked Odysseus. "I have never heard about it."

"When Heracles was a fair-faced youth, and life was all before him, he went out one morning to do an errand for his stepfather Amphitryon. But as he walked, his heart was full of bitter thoughts; and he murmured because others no better than himself were living in ease and pleasure, while for him there was naught but a life of labor and pain. And as he thought upon these things, he came to a place where two roads met; and he stopped, not certain which one to take. The road on his right was hilly and rough; there was no beauty in it or about it: but he saw that it led straight towards the blue mountains in the far distance. The road on his left was broad and smooth, with shade trees on either side, where sang an innumerable choir of birds; and it went winding among green meadows, where bloomed countless flowers: but it ended in fog and mist long before it ever reached the wonderful blue mountains in the distance.

"While the lad stood in doubt as to these roads, he saw two fair women coming towards him, each on a different road. The one who came by the flowery way reached him first, and Heracles saw that she was beautiful as a summer day. Her cheeks were red, her eyes sparkled; she spoke warm, persuasive words. 'O noble youth, she said, 'be no longer bowed down with labor and sore trials, but come and follow me. I will lead you into pleasant paths, where there are no storms to disturb and no troubles to annoy. You shall live in ease, with one unending round of music and mirth; and you shall not want for any thing that makes life joyous,—sparkling wine, or soft couches, or rich robes, or the loving eyes of beautiful maidens. Come with me, and life shall be to you a day-dream of gladness.'

"By this time the other fair woman had drawn near, and she now spoke to the lad. 'I have nothing to promise you,' said she, 'save that which you shall win with your own strength. The road upon which I would lead you is uneven and hard, and climbs many a hill, and descends into many a valley and quagmire. The views which you will sometimes get from the hilltops are grand and glorious, but the deep valleys are dark, and the ascent from them is toilsome; but the road leads to the blue mountains of endless fame, which you see far away on the horizon. They cannot be reached without labor; in fact, there is nothing worth having that must not be won by toil. If you would have fruits and flowers, you must plant them and care for them; if you would gain the love of your fellow-men, you must love them and suffer for them; if you would enjoy the favor of Heaven, you must make yourself worthy of that favor; if you would have eternal fame, you must not scorn the hard road that leads to it.'

"Then Heracles saw that this lady, although she was as beautiful as the other, had a countenance pure and gentle, like the sky on a balmy morning in May.

" 'What is your name?' he asked.

" 'Some call me Labor,' she answered, 'but others know me as Virtue.'

"Then he turned to the first lady. 'And what is your name?' he asked.

" 'Some call me Pleasure,' she said, with a bewitching smile, but I choose to be known as the Joyous and Happy One.'

" 'Virtue,' said Heracles, 'I will take thee as my guide! The road of labor and honest effort shall be mine, and my heart shall no longer cherish bitterness or discontent.'

"And he put his hand into that of Virtue, and entered with her upon the straight and forbidding road which leads to the fair blue mountains in the pale and distant horizon.

"My dear grandson, make thou the same wise choice.

"But now the fire has burned low, and it is time that both old and young should seek repose. Go now to your chamber and your couch; and pleasant dreams be yours until the new day dawns, bringing its labors and its victories."

TWO FAMOUS BOAR HUNTS

HARDLY had the morning tinged the eastern sky with her yellow light, when Odysseus arose from his couch, and quickly clothed himself; for he had been awakened by the sound of hurrying feet, and many voices, and the barking of dogs, beneath his chamber window. When he went down into the great hall, he was greeted by his six stalwart uncles, all of whom were dressed for the chase, and armed with spears and knives.

"To-day we hunt the wild boar on the wooded slopes of Parnassus," said Echion, the eldest. "How glad we should be if you were old enough and strong enough to join us in the sport!"

The heart of Odysseus was stirred at once, like that of a warrior when he hears the battle-call. "I am certainly strong enough!" he cried. "I will ask my grandfather if I may go."

Autolycus smiled when the boy made known his wish. Indeed, he was expecting such a request, and would have been disappointed and displeased if it had not been made.

"Yes, go, my child," he said; "and while I sit here, bound with the fetters of old age, my blessing shall go with you."

Odysseus thanked his grandfather, and lost no time in making himself ready for the hunt. A hasty meal was eaten; and then the huntsmen, with a great number of dogs and serving-men, sallied forth, and began to climb the mountain slopes. The master of the hunt was an old, gray-bearded man, one of the last of the ancient race of heroes, whose whole life had been spent in the household of Autolycus. Old as he was, he outstrode all the other huntsmen; but Odysseus, young and supple, kept close behind him,—a dwarf following in the wake of a giant. Upward and still upward they toiled, while their comrades, with the hounds, followed slowly far below them. They passed through the belt of pine trees, and left the wooded slopes behind. There was now nothing but bare rocks before and above them. The cold winds whistled about their heads; the mountain eagles soared and screamed in the sharp morning air.

"Surely, my father," said Odysseus, "the lair of the wild boar cannot be on these bleak heights. Would it not be better to seek him among the woods of the lower slopes?"

"You are right," said the old man, stopping at last upon one of the highest crags. "I have brought you to this spot, not in search of game, but to show you what is a truly great and beautiful sight. Your tutor has told me that you once had a glimpse of the world from Mount Neritus; now look around you, and see the world itself!"

Then the lad looked; and far away on the blue horizon he saw the silvery heights of Olympus, the throne of mighty Zeus glittering in the sunlight, and canopied with clouds. On his right he beheld Mount Helicon and the fruitful plains of Bœotia, and the blue sea of Ægæa stretching away and away towards the sunrise halls of Helios. Southward lay the Bay of Crissa, and beyond it the land of mighty Pelops, and busy Corinth, and the rich pasture-lands of Arcadia, Then turning to the west, he saw, like a mere speck on the horizon, his own loved Ithaca; while nearer were the woods of Calydon and the green headlands of Achaia. At that moment the clouds which had been hanging about the mountain-top suddenly melted away, and the sun shone out bright and clear, bathing the woods and crags in purple and gold; while at the same time the music of ten thousand voices of birds and beasts and nymphs and waterfalls was borne up from below to their delighted ears.

"Is not this a beautiful world?" asked the aged hero, baring his gray head to the cold winds. "What would you not give to have it all for your own?"

The lad answered not a word; but his eyes filled with tears as he thought of his home and of those whom he loved, far away by the green slopes of little Neritus.

"My son," then said the hero, "remember the choice of Heracles. Happiness is to be gotten from within us. It is not to be bought with silver and gold, nor yet is it to be seized upon with violence. Better have a clean conscience than to own all Hellas; better—But hark! I hear the dogs in the dells far below us! Let us hasten down, for they have started the game."

Within a thorny thicket where grew the vines and leaves so closely that the sun's rays never struggled through them, the huge wild boar had made his lair. Hither the hounds had tracked him; and their deep baying, and the trampling of many feet among the dead leaves upon the ground, had roused the beast, and stirred him into fury. Suddenly he sprang from his lair, and gnashing his huge tusks, and foaming with fury, he charged upon his foes. The dogs fell back, afraid to come too close to an enemy so fierce and strong; and with their many-toned bays they made the echoes of Parnassus ring.

Just at this moment, the boy Odysseus rushed down into the glen, his long spear poised and ready to strike. But the great beast waited not for the stroke: he dashed furiously at the boy, who quickly leaped aside, although too late. The boar's sharp tusk struck Odysseus just above the knee, cutting a fearful gash, tearing the flesh, and even grazing the bone. But the lad, undaunted, struck manfully with his weapon. The bright spear was driven straight to the heart of the beast; with one great cry he fell, and gnashing his huge jaws helplessly he died among the withered leaves. The boy, faint with pain and the joy of victory, staggered into the arms of his stalwart uncles, who had hastened to succor him. Gently they bound up the ghastly wound, and with charms and witchery stanched the flowing blood. Then, upon a litter woven of vines and pliant twigs, they bore him down the deep glen to the broad halls of old Autolycus; and the men and boys, having flayed the grisly beast, brought afterward its head and bristly hide, and set them up as trophies in the gateway.

For many weary days, Odysseus lay helpless on a couch of pain. But his kind kinsmen, and Phemius his tutor, waited on him tenderly, and his fair grandmother Amphithea nursed him. And when the pain left him, and he began to grow strong again, he loved to lie on the bearskins at his grandfather's feet, and listen to tales of the earlier days, when the older race of heroes walked the earth.

"When I was younger than I am to-day," said the old chief, as they sat one evening in the light of the blazing brands,—"when I was much younger than now, it was my fortune to take part in the most famous boar hunt the world has ever known.

"There lived at that time, in Calydon, a mighty chief named Oineus,—and, indeed, I know not but that he still lives. Oineus was rich in vineyards and in orchards, and no other man in all Ætolia was happier or more blessed than he. He had married, early in life, the princess Althea, fairest of the Acarnanian maidens; and to them a son had been born, golden-haired and beautiful, whom they called Meleager.

"When Meleager was yet but one day old, his father held him in his arms, and prayed to Zeus and the ever-living powers above: 'Grant, Father Zeus, and all ye deathless ones, that this my son may be the foremost among the men of Hellas. And let it come to pass, that when they see his valiant deeds, his countrymen shall say, 'Behold, this youth is greater than his father,' and all of one accord shall hail him as their guardian king.'

"Then his mother Althea, weeping tears of joy, prayed to Pallas Athené, that the boy might grow up to be pure-minded and gentle, the hope and pride of his parents, and the delight and staff of their declining years. Scarcely had the words of prayer died from her lips, when there came into her chamber the three unerring Fates who spin the destinies of men. White-robed and garlanded, they stood beside the babe, and with unwearied fingers drew out the lines of his untried life. Sad Clotho held the golden distaff in her hand, and twirled and twisted the delicate thread. Lachesis, now sad, now hopeful, with her long white fingers held the hourglass, and framed her lips to say, 'It is enough.' And Atropos, blind and unpitying as the future always is, stood ready, with cruel shears, to clip the twist in twain. Busily and silently sad Clotho spun; and the golden thread, thin as a spider's web, yet beautiful as a sunbeam, grew longer and more golden between her skilful fingers. Then Lachesis cried out, 'It is finished!' But Atropos hid her shears beneath her mantle, and said, 'Not so. Behold, there is a brand burning upon the hearth. Wait until it is all burned into ashes and smoke, and then I will cut the thread of the child's life. Spin on, sweet Clotho!'

"Quick as thought, Althea sprang forward, snatched the blazing brand from the hearth, and quenched its flame in a jar of water; and when she knew that not a single spark was left glowing upon it, she locked it safely in a chest where none but she could find it. As she did this, the pitiless sisters vanished from her sight, saying as they flitted through the air, 'We bide our time.'

"Meleager grew up to be a tall and fair and gentle youth; and when at last he became a man, he sailed on the ship Argo, with Jason, and Laertes your father, and the great heroes of that day, to far-off Colchis, in search of the Golden Fleece. Many brave deeds were his in foreign lands; and when he came home again to Calydon, he brought with him a fair young wife, gentle Cleopatra, daughter of Idas the boaster.

"Oineus had gathered in his harvest; and he was glad and thankful in his heart, because his fields had yielded plenteously; his vines had been loaded with purple grapes, and his orchards filled with abundance of pleasant fruit. Grateful, as men should always be, to the givers of peace and plenty, he held within his halls a harvest festival to which the brave and beautiful of all Ætolia came. Happy was this feast, and the hours were bright with smiles and sunshine; and men forgot sorrow and labor, and thought only of the gladness of life.

"Then Oineus took of the first-fruits of his fields and vineyards and his orchards, and offered them in thankful offerings to the givers of good. But he forgot to deck the shrine of Artemis with gifts, little thinking the arrow-darting queen cared for any thing which mortal men might offer her. Ah, woful mistake was that! For, in her anger at the slight, Artemis sent a savage boar, with ivory tusks and foaming mouth, to overrun the lands of Calydon. Many a field did the monster ravage, many a tree uproot; and all the growing vines, which late had borne so rich a vintage, were trampled to the ground. Sadly troubled was Oineus, and the chieftains of Ætolia knew not what to do. For the fierce beast could not be slain, but with his terrible tusks he had sent many a rash hunter to an untimely death. Then the young man Meleager said, 'I will call together the heroes of Hellas, and we will hunt the boar in the woods of Calydon.'

"And so at the call of Meleager, the warriors flocked from every land, to join in the hunt of the fierce wild boar. Among them came Castor and Polydeuces, the twin brothers from Lacedæmon; and Idas the boaster, father-in-law of Meleager, from Messene; and mighty Jason, captain of the Argo; and Atalanta, the swift-footed daughter of Iasus of Arcadia; and many Acarnanian huntsmen lent by the sons of Thestios, Althea's brothers. Thither also did I, Autolycus, hasten, although men spitefully said that I was far more skilful in taking tame beasts than in slaying wild ones.

"Nine days we feasted in the halls of Oineus; and every day we tried our skill with bows and arrows, and tested the strength of our well-seasoned spears. On the tenth, the bugles sounded, and hounds and huntsmen gathered in the courtyard of the chief, chafing for the hunt. But a proud fellow named Cepheus, of Arcadia, when he saw fair Atalanta equipped for the chase, drew back disdainfully, and said,—

" 'In my country, it is not the custom for heroes to go to battle or to hunt side by side with women. Woman's place is at home: her weapons are the distaff and the needle; her duty is to practise well the household virtues. If you allow this young girl to join in this hunt, then I will turn my face homeward, and seek in the Arcadian land adventures worthy of men.'

"Then Meleager angrily answered, 'In the Arcadian land, if report speaks truly, the deeds deemed worthiest of men are the watching of flocks, and the tuning of the shepherd's pipe. It is fear, not bravery, that makes you seek an excuse to leave the chase of the wild boar before it is begun. You are afraid of the beast; and you are still more afraid of the maiden Atalanta, lest she should prove to be more skilled than you. Have you heard how, when an infant, she was left to perish on the Parthenian hill, and would have died, had not a she-bear cared for her until some hunters rescued her? Have you heard how, as she grew up, her beauty was greater than that of any other maiden, and how no one but

Artemis, the archer-queen, could shoot the swift arrow so fair and straight? Have you heard what she did on the ship Argo, when, with Jason as our captain, we sailed to the utmost bounds of the earth, and brought home with us the fleece of gold? Have you heard how, with her own arrows, she slew the beastly centaurs, Rhœcus and Hylæus, because they dared to make love to one so pure and beautiful? Doubtless you have heard all these things, and you are afraid to go to the field of danger with one so much nobler than yourself. Go back, then, to your sheep-tending Arcadia! No one will miss you in the chase.'

"Then Cepheus blushed, but more from shame than anger. 'I will ride with you into the wood,' said he, 'and never again shall any man accuse me of having a timid heart.'

"Soon we sallied forth from the town, a hundred huntsmen, with dogs innumerable. Through the fields and orchards, laid waste by the savage beast, we passed; and Atalanta, keen of sight and swift of foot, her long hair floating in the wind behind her, led all the rest. It was not long until, in a narrow dell once green with vines and trees, but now strewn thick with withered branches, we roused the fierce creature from his lair. At first he fled, followed closely by the baying hounds. Then suddenly he faced his foes; with gnashing teeth and bloodshot eyes, he charged furiously upon them. A score of hounds were slain outright; and Cepheus, rushing blindly onward, was caught by the beast, and torn in pieces by his sharp tusks. Brave Peleus of Phthia with unsteady aim let fly an arrow from his bow, which, falling short of the mark, smote his friend Eurytion full in the breast, and stretched him lifeless upon the ground. Then swift-footed Atalanta, bounding forward, struck the beast a deadly blow with her spear. He stopped short his furious onslaught; and Amphiaraus, the hero and prophet of Argos, launching a swift arrow, put out one of his eyes. Terrible were the cries of the wounded creature, as, blinded and bleeding, he made a last charge upon the huntsmen. But Meleager with a skilful sword-thrust pierced his heart, and the beast fell weltering in his gore. Great joy filled the hearts of the Calydonians, when they saw the scourge of their land laid low and helpless. They quickly flayed the beast, and the heroes who had shared in the hunt divided the flesh among them; but the head and the bristly hide they gave to Meleager.

" 'Not to me does the prize belong,' he cried, 'but to Atalanta, the swift-footed huntress. For the first wound—the true death-stroke, indeed—was given by her; and to her, woman though she be, all honor and the prize must be awarded.'

"With these words, he bore the grinning head and the bristly hide to the fair young huntress, and laid them at her feet. Then his uncles, the sons of Acarnanian Thestios, rushed angrily forward, saying that no woman should ever bear a prize away from them; and they seized the hide, and would have taken it away, had not Meleager forbidden them. Yet they would not loose their hold upon the prize, but drew their swords, and wrathfully threatened Meleager's life. The hero's heart grew hot within him, and he shrunk not from the affray. Long and fearful was the struggle,—uncles against nephew; but in the end the sons of Thestios lay bleeding upon the ground, while the victor brought again the boar's hide, and laid it the second time at Atalanta's feet. The fair huntress took the prize, and carried it away with her to deck her father's hall in the pleasant Arcadian land. And the heroes, when they had feasted nine other days with King Oineus, betook themselves to their own homes.

"But the hearts of the Acarnanians were bitter towards Meleager, because of the death of the sons of Thestios, and because no part of the wild boar was awarded to them. They called their chiefs around them, and all their brave men, and made war upon King Oineus and Meleager. Many battles did they fight round Calydon, and among the Ætolian hills; yet while Meleager led his warriors to the fray, the Acarnanians fared but ill.

"Then Queen Althea, filled with grief for her brothers' untimely death, forgot her love for her son, and prayed that her Acarnanian kinsmen might prevail against him. Upon the hard earth she knelt: she beat the ground with her hands, and heaped the dust about her; and, weeping bitter tears, she called upon Hades and heartless Persephone to avenge her of Meleager. And even as she prayed, the pitiless

Furies, wandering amid the darkness, heard her cries, and came, obedient to her wishes.

"When Meleager heard that his mother had turned against him, he withdrew in sorrow to his own house, and sought comfort and peace with his wife, fair Cleopatra; and he would not lead his warriors any more to battle against the Acarnanians. Then the enemy besieged the city: a fearful tumult rose about the gates; the high towers were assaulted, and everywhere the Calydonians were driven back dismayed and beaten. With uplifted hands and tearful eyes, King Oineus and the elders of the city came to Meleager, and besought him to take the field again. Rich gifts they offered him. They bade him choose for his own the most fertile farm in Calydon,—at the least fifty acres, half for tillage and half for vines; but he would not listen to them. The din of battle thickened outside the gates; the towers shook with the thundering blows of the besiegers. Old Oineus with trembling limbs climbed up the stairway to his son's secluded chamber, and, weeping, prayed him to come down and save the city from fire and pillage. Still he kept silent, and went not. His sisters came, and his most trusted friends. 'Come, Meleager,' they prayed, 'forget thy grief, and think only of our great need. Aid thy people, or we shall all perish!'

"None of these prayers moved him. The gates were beaten down; the enemy was within the walls; the tide of battle shook the very tower where

Meleager sat; the doom of Calydon seemed to be sealed. Then came the fair Cleopatra, and knelt before her husband, and besought him to withhold no longer the aid which he alone could give. 'O Meleager,' she sobbed, 'none but thou can save us. Wilt thou sit still, and see the city laid in ashes, thy dearest friends slaughtered, and thy wife and sweet babes dragged from their homes and sold into cruel slavery?'

"Then Meleager rose, and girded on his armor. To the streets he hastened, shouting his well-known battle-cry. Eagerly and hopefully did the Calydonian warriors rally around him. Fiercely did they meet the foe. Terrible was the bloodshed. Back from the battered gates and the crumbling wall, the Acarnanian hosts were driven. A panic seized upon them. They turned and fled, and not many of them escaped the swords of Meleager's men.

"Again there was peace in Calydon, and the orchards of King Oineus blossomed and bore fruit as of old; but the gifts and large rewards which the elders had promised to Meleager were forgotten. He had saved his country, but his countrymen were ungrateful.

"Then Meleager again laid aside his war-gear, and sought the quiet of his own home, and the cheering presence of fair Cleopatra. For the remembrance of his mother's curse and his country's ingratitude weighed heavily on his mind, and he cared no longer to mingle with his fellow-men.

"Then it was that Althea's hatred of her son waxed stronger, and she thought of the half-burnt brand which she had hidden, and of the words which the fatal sisters had spoken so many years before.

" 'He is no longer my son,' said she, 'and why should I withhold the burning of the brand? He can never again bring comfort to my heart; for the blood of my brothers, whom I loved, is upon his head.'

"And she took the charred billet from the place where she had hidden it, and cast it again into the flames. And as it slowly burned away, so did the life of Meleager wane. Lovingly he bade his wife farewell; softly he whispered a prayer to the unseen powers above; and as the flickering flames of the fatal brand died into darkness, he gently breathed his last.

"Then sharp-toothed remorse seized upon Althea, and the mother-love which had slept in her bosom was re-awakened. Too late, also, the folk of Calydon remembered who it was who had saved them from slavery and death. Down into the comfortless halls of Hades, Althea hastened to seek her son's forgiveness. The loving heart of Cleopatra, surcharged with grief, was broken; and her gentle spirit fled to the world of shades to meet that of her hero-husband. And Meleager's sisters would not be consoled, so great was the sorrow which had come upon them; and they wept and lamented day and night, until kind Artemis in pity for their youth changed them into the birds which we call Meleagrides."

Lying on the bearskins at his grandfather's feet, and listening to stories like this, Odysseus did not feel that time was burdensome. The wound upon his knee healed slowly; and when at last he could walk again, a white scar, as long and as broad as a finger, told the story of his combat with the fierce wild boar. By this time the summer was far spent, and the bard Phemius was impatient to return to Ithaca.

"The grapes in your father's vineyard are growing purple, and his orchards are laden with ripening fruit," said he to Odysseus; "and the days are near at hand when your anxious mother will gaze with longing over the sea, expecting your return."

But there was no vessel at the port on the bay to carry them home by the nearest way; and days and months might pass ere any ship, sent thither by Laertes, would arrive. How, then, were they to return to Ithaca?

"Here is your uncle, bold Echion, who goes to-morrow to Iolcos by the sea, carrying gifts and a message from Autolycus to old King Peleus. We will go with him."

"But Iolcos is farther still from Ithaca," said Odysseus.

"True," answered Phemius. "But from Iolcos, at this season of the year, there are many vessels sailing to Corinth and the islands of the sea. Once at Corinth, and we shall find no lack of ships to carry us across the bay of Crissa to our own loved Ithaca."

And thus the journey home was planned. It was a long and devious route by way of Iolcos and the Eubœan Sea; and no one could say how many dangers they might meet, or how many delays they should encounter. Yet nothing better could be done, if they would return before the summer ended.

The great Autolycus blessed Odysseus on departing, and gave him rich gifts of gold and priceless gems, and many words of sage advice. "I shall see thee no more," he said; "but thy name shall be spoken countless ages hence, and men shall say, 'How shrewd and far-seeing, brave in war, and wise in counsel, was Odysseus!'"

ADVENTURE VII

AT OLD CHEIRON'S SCHOOL

AFTER a long, hard journey by land and sea, Odysseus and his tutor, with bold Echion, came to Iolcos. Aged Peleus, king of Phthia and the fertile plains of Iolcos, greeted them with show of heartiest welcome; for he remembered that Laertes had been his friend and comrade long years before, when together on the Argo they sailed the briny deep, and he was glad to see the son of that old comrade; and he took Odysseus by the hand, and led him into his palace, and gave him of the best of all that he had.

"Tarry with me for a month," he said. "My ships are now at sea, but they will return; and when the moon rises again full and round, as it did last night, I will send you safe to Corinth on the shores of the Bay of Crissa."

And so Odysseus and the bard staid a whole month at Iolcos, in the house of Peleus the king. There were feasting and merriment in the halls every day; and yet time hung heavily, for the boy longed to re-behold his own loved Ithaca, and could hardly wait to see the moon grow full and round again.

"What mountain is that which looms up so grandly on our left, and whose sides seem covered with dark forests?" asked Odysseus one day, as he walked with his tutor beside the sea.

"It is famous Mount Pelion," said the bard; "and that other mountain with the steeper sides, which stands out faintly against the far horizon, is the scarcely less famed Ossa."

"I have heard my father speak of piling Pelion upon Ossa," said Odysseus, "but I cannot understand how that can be done."

"There were once two brothers, the tallest that the grain-giving earth has ever reared," said Phemius. "Their names were Otus and Ephialtes; and they threatened to make war even against the deathless ones who dwell on Mount Olympus. They boasted that they would pile Ossa on Olympus, and Pelion, with all its woods, upon the top of Ossa, that so they might make a pathway to the sky. And, had they lived to manhood's years, no one can say what deeds they would have done. But silver-bowed Apollo, with his swift arrows, slew the twain ere yet the down had bloomed upon their cheeks or darkened their chins with the promise of manhood. And so Pelion still stands beside the sea, and Ossa, in its own place, guards the lovely vale of Tempe."

"Oh, now I remember something else about Mount Pelion," cried Odysseus. "It was from the trees which grew upon its sides, that the ship Argo was built. And I have heard my father tell how Cheiron the Centaur once lived in a cave on Pelion, and taught the young heroes who came to learn of him; and how young Jason came down the mountain one day, and boldly stood before King Pelias, who had robbed old Æson, his father, of the kingdom which was rightfully his. Would that I had been one of Cheiron's pupils, and had shared the instruction which he gave to those youthful heroes!"

"The old Centaur still lives in his cave on Mount Pelion," said Phemius. "To-morrow, if King Peleus is willing, we will go and see him."

And so, the next day, the two went out of Iolcos, through vineyards and fields and olive orchards, towards Pelion, the snow-crowned warder of the shore. They followed a winding pathway, and came ere long to the foot of the mighty mountain. Above them were frowning rocks, and dark forests of pine, which seemed ready to fall upon and crush them. But among the trees, and in the crannies of the rocks, there grew thousands of sweetest flowers, and every kind of health-giving herb, and tender grass for the mountain-climbing deer. Up and up they climbed, until the dark forests gave place to stunted shrubs, and the shrubs to barren rocks. Then the pathway led downward again to the head of a narrow glen, where roared a foaming waterfall. There they came to the mouth of a cave opening out upon a sunny ledge, and almost hidden behind a broad curtain of blossoming vines. From within the cave there came the sound of music,—the sweet tones of a harp, mingled with the voices of singers.

Of what did they sing?

They sang of things pure and good and beautiful,—of the mighty sea, and the grain-bearing earth, and the blue vault of heaven; of faith, strong and holy; of hope, bright and trustful; of love, pure and mighty. Then the singing ceased, and the harp was laid aside.

Odysseus and the bard went quickly forward, and stood waiting beside the wide-open door. They could see, by looking in, that the low walls of the cave were adorned with shields of leather or bronze, with the antlers of deer, and with many other relics of battle or of the chase. Upon the smooth white floor were soft couches of bearskins; and upon the hearth stone in the centre blazed a bright fire of twigs, casting a ruddy, flickering light into the farthest nook and cranny of that strange room.

They had not long to wait at the door. An old man with white hair, and beard reaching to his waist, with eyes as clear and bright as those of a falcon, and with a step as firm as that of youth, came quickly forward to greet them. Odysseus thought that he had never seen a man with so noble and yet so sad a mien.

"Hail, strangers!" said the aged hero, taking their hands. "Hail, son of Laertes—for I know thee!—welcome to the home of Cheiron, the last of his race! Come in, and you shall be kindly entertained; and after you have rested your weary limbs, you shall tell me why you have come to Pelion, and what favor you have to ask of me."

Therewith he turned again into the broad cave-hall, and Odysseus and his tutor followed him. And he led his guests, and seated them on pleasant couches not far from the glowing fire upon the hearth. Then a comely youth brought water in a stone pitcher, and poured it in a basin, that they might wash their hands. And another lad brought wheaten bread, and set it by them on a polished table; and another brought golden honey in the honeycomb, and many other dainties, and laid them on the board. And when they were ready, a fourth lad lifted and placed before them a platter of venison, and cups full of ice-cold water from the mountain cataract. While they sat, partaking of these bounties, not a word was spoken in the cave; for old Cheiron never forgot the courtesy due to guests and strangers. When they had finished, he bade them stay a while upon the couches where they sat; and he took a golden lyre in his hands, and deftly touched the chords, bringing forth the most restful music that Odysseus had ever heard. He played a soft, low melody which seemed to carry their minds far away into a summerland of peace, where they wandered at will by the side of still waters, and through sunlit fields and groves, and reposed under the shelter of calm blue skies, shielded by the boundless love of the unknown Creator. When he had finished, Odysseus thought no more of the toilsome journey from Iolcos, or of the wearisome climbing of the mountain: he thought only of the wise and wonderful old man who sat before him.

"Now tell me," said Cheiron, laying his lyre aside,—"tell me what errand brings you hither, and what I can do to aid you."

"We have no errand," answered Phemius, "save to see one of the immortals, and to listen to the words of wisdom and beauty which fall from his lips. We know that you have been the friend and teacher of heroes such as have not had their peers on earth; and this lad Odysseus, who is himself the son of a hero, would fain learn something from you."

Cheiron smiled, and looked full into the young lad's face.

"I have trained many such youths as you for the battle of life," he said. "And your father, as were all the Argonauts, was well known to me. You are welcome to Mount Pelion, and to old Cheiron's school. But why do you look at my feet?"

Odysseus blushed, but could make no answer.

"I understand it," said Cheiron, speaking in a tone of sadness. "You expected to find me half man, half horse, and you were looking for the hoofs; for thus have many men thought concerning me and my race. Long time ago my people dwelt in the valleys and upon the plains of Thessaly; and they were the first who tamed the wild horses of the desert flats, and taught them to obey the hand of their riders. For untold years my fathers held this land, and they were as free as the winds which play upon the top of Pelion. Their warriors, galloping on their swift horses with their long lances ready in their hands, knew no fear, nor met any foe that could stand against them; and hence men called them Centaurs, the piercers of the air. But by and by there came a strong people from beyond the sea, who built houses of stone, and lived in towns; and these made cruel war upon the swift-riding Centaurs. They were the Lapiths, the stone-persuaders, and they had never seen or heard of horses; and for a long time they fancied that our warriors were monsters, half-steed, half-man, living wild among the mountains and upon the plain. And so the story has gone abroad throughout the world, that all the Centaurs, and even I, the last of the race, are hardly human, but have hoofs and manes, and live as horses live.

"Long and sad was the war between the Centaurs and the Lapiths; but the stone-persuaders were stronger than the piercers of the air. In time, my people were driven into the mountains, where they lived as wild men in the caves, and in the sunless gorges and ravines; and their enemies, the Lapiths, abode in the rich valleys, and held the broad pasture-lands which had once been ours. Then it chanced that Peirithous, king of the Lapiths, saw Hippodameia, fairest of our mountain maidens, and wished to wed her. Whether her father consented to the marriage, or whether the Lapiths carried her away by force, I cannot tell; but Peirithous made a great wedding feast, and to it he invited the chiefs of the Centaurs, and great Theseus of Athens, and

Nestor of sandy Pylos, and many others of the noblest heroes of Hellas. Many wild and dark stories have been told of what happened at that wedding feast; but you must remember that all these stories have come from the mouths of our enemies, the stone-persuading Lapiths, and that their truth may well be doubted. Let me tell you about it, as I understand the facts to be:—

"In the midst of the feast, when the Lapiths were drunken with wine, Eurytion, the boldest of the Centaurs, rose quickly to his feet, and beckoned to his fellows. Without a word they seized upon the bride; they carried her, not unwilling, from the hall; they seated her upon a swift steed which stood ready at the door; then in hot haste they mounted, aiming to ride with their prize back to their mountain homes. But the Lapiths were aroused, and rushed from the hall ere our horsemen were outside of the gates. Fearful was the struggle which followed. Our men were armed with pine clubs only, which they had hidden beneath their cloaks, for they dared not bring weapons to the wedding feast. The Lapiths fought with spears; and with pitiless hate they slew one after another of the Centaurs, until hardly a single man escaped to the mountains. But the war ended not with that; for Peirithous, burning with anger, drove the remnant of people out of their mountain homes, and forced them to flee far away to the lonely land of Pindus; and I, alone of all my race, was left in my cavern-dwelling on the wooded slopes of Pelion."

When Cheiron had ended his story, Odysseus saw that his eyes were filled with tears, and that his hand trembled as he reached again for his lyre, and played a short, sad melody, as mournful as a funeral song.

"Why did you not go with your kindred to the land of Pindus?" asked Phemius.

"This is my home," answered Cheiron. "The fair valley which you see yonder was once my father's pasture land. All the country that lies before us, even to the meeting of the earth and the sky, is the country of my forefathers. I have neither parents, nor brothers, nor wife, nor children. Why should I wish to go away from all that is dear to me? This is a pleasant place, and the young boys who have been my pupils have made my life very happy."

"Please tell us about your pupils," said Odysseus, moving nearer to the wise old man.

"So many boys have been under my care," said Cheiron, "that I could not tell you about them all. Some have come and been taught, and gone back to their homes; and the world has never heard of them, because their lots have been cast in pleasant places, and their lives have been spent in peace. There have been others who have made their names famous upon the earth; for their paths were beset with difficulties, and before them loomed great mountains which they must needs remove or be crushed by them. Among these latter were Heracles, doomed to a life of labor, because another had usurped the place which he should have had; young

88

Jason, hiding from the cruel hatred of his uncle Pelias; and gentle Asclepius, bereft of a mother's love, and cast friendless upon the world's cold mercies. And there were also Peleus my grandson, who is now your host at Iolcos; and Actæon, the famous hunter; and many of the heroes who afterward sailed on the Argo, to the golden strand of Colchis. Each of these lads had a mind of his own, and tastes which it was for me to foster and to train. Heracles was headstrong, selfish, impulsive,— terrible when he did not bridle his passions; and yet his great heart was full of love for the poor, the weak, and the down-trodden, and he studied to make plans for lightening their burdens. Jason loved the water; and wrapped in his cloak, he would sit for hours on Pelion's top, and gaze with longing eyes upon the purple sea. Asclepius delighted to wander among the crags and in the ravines of Pelion, gathering herbs and flowers, and studying the habits of birds and beasts. And Actæon had a passion for the woods and the fields, and had ever a pack of swift hounds at his heels, ready for the chase of wild boar or mountain deer.

"When these lads came to me, I saw that I must give to each the food which was best fitted for his needs, and which his mind most craved. Had I dealt with all alike, and taught all the same lessons, I doubt if any would have grown to manhood's full estate. But, while I curbed the headstrong will of Heracles, I did what I could to foster his love of virtue and his inventive genius; I taught young Jason all that I knew about this wonderful earth, and the

seas and islands which lie around it; I led Asclepius
farther along the pathway which he had chosen, and
showed him the virtues that were hidden in plants
and flowers; I went with Actæon upon the chase,
and taught him that there is no sport in cruelty, and
that the life of the weakest creature should not be
taken without good cause. Thus I moulded the mind
of each of the lads according to its bent; and each
one grew in stature and in strength and in beauty,
before my eyes. And then there were general lessons
which I gave to them all, leading them to the
knowledge of those things which are necessary to
the well-equipped and perfect man of our day. I
taught them how to wield the weapons of warfare
and of the chase; how to ride and to swim; and how
to bear fatigue without murmuring, and face danger
without fear. And I showed them how to take care
of their own bodies, so that they might be strong
and graceful, and full of health and vigor; and I
taught them how to heal diseases, and how to treat
wounds, and how to nurse the sick. And, more than
all else, I taught them to reverence and love that
great Power, so little understood by us, but whom
mankind will someday learn to know.

"It was not long till Heracles went out in his
might to rid the world of monsters, to defend the
innocent and the helpless, and to set right that which
is wrong; and, for aught I know, he is toiling still
along the straight road of Virtue, towards the blue
mountains of Fame. And Jason, as you know, left
me, and went down to Iolcos, to claim his birthright
of old Pelias; and being bidden to bring the Golden

Fleece to Hellas, he built the Argo, and sailed with the heroes to far-away Colchis. It was a proud day for me, his old teacher, when he came back to Iolcos with the glittering treasure; and I trusted that a life of happiness and glory was before him. But, alas! he had forgotten my teaching, and had joined himself to evil; and Medea the witch, whom he loved, brought untold misery upon his head, and drove him ere long to an untimely death.

"Then Asclepius went out upon his mission; everywhere that he went, he healed and purified and raised and blessed. He was the greatest conqueror among all my pupils; but he won, not by strength like Heracles, nor by guile like Jason, but through gentleness and sympathy and brotherly love, and by knowledge and skill and patient self-sacrifice; and to him men gave the highest honor, because he cured while others killed. But the powers of darkness are ever hateful towards the good; and Hades, when he saw that Asclepius snatched back to life even those who were at death's door, complained that the great healer was robbing his kingdom. And men say that Zeus hearkened to this complaint, and that he smote Asclepius with his thunderbolts. Then the face of the sun was veiled in sorrow, and men and beasts and all creatures upon the earth wept for great grief, and the trees dropped their leaves to the ground, and the flowers closed their petals and withered upon their stalks, because the gentle physician, who had cured all pains and sickness, was no longer in the land of the living. And the wrath of silver-bowed Apollo was stirred within him, and he went down to the great

91

smithy of Hephaestus, and, with his swift arrows, slew the Cyclopes who had forged the thunderbolts for Zeus, and spared not one. Then Zeus in his turn was filled with anger; and he sent the golden-haired Apollo to Pherae, in Thessaly, to serve for a whole year as bondsman to King Admetus."

At this moment, a tall and very handsome lad, whom Odysseus had not yet seen, came into the room. He was not more than six years old; his long amber hair fell in waves upon his shoulders; his eyes twinkled and flashed like the sunlight on the blue sea waves; he held his head erect, and he walked with a noble grace which betokened the proud soul within his breast. The eyes of Odysseus were fixed upon him, and he wondered who this noble human being could be. Cheiron saw his questioning look, and called the young lad to him.

"Odysseus," said he, "this is my great-grandchild, young Achilles, the son of King Peleus your host. Something tells me that your life and his will in aftertimes be strangely mingled; whether as friends or as foes, I cannot tell. You shall be friends to-day, at least, and after a while you shall go out together, and try your skill at archery. But, Achilles, you may go now and play with your fellows: I have something more to say to young Odysseus."

The lad turned, and left the room as gracefully as he had entered. Then Cheiron turned again to Odysseus and the bard.

"I was telling you about my pupils," he said; "and I will speak of but one other, for there are reasons why you should know his history. Peleus, the son of Æacus and my loved daughter Endeis, was brought to me by his mother from Ægina. There was something in the boy's face which showed that a strange, sad life was to be his; and, although he was not a promising lad, yet when he left me to go with Jason to Colchis, I felt great grief at losing him. But by and by, after the heroes had returned, I heard that Peleus had done many wicked things in Ægina, and that he had been driven into exile for his crimes. He went first to Ceyx in Thessaly, a lonely wanderer, cast off and forsaken by all his friends. And a story is told, that in his loneliness and his sorrow, he one day prayed to Zeus that he would give him companions. And Zeus heard his prayer, and great armies of ants were changed at once into men; and they did homage to Peleus, and became his subjects, and hence he is still called the King of the Myrmidons. Then he went to Phthia where Eurytion reigned. And Eurytion purified him from his crimes, and gave him his daughter Antigone in wedlock, and with her the third of his kingdom. But in an evil day they hunted the wild boar together in the woods of Calydon, and Peleus unwittingly slew his friend with an ill-aimed arrow. Then he fled from the people of Phthia, and came to Iolcos, where Acastus, the son of old Pelias, ruled. And Acastus welcomed him kindly, and purified him from the stain of Eurytion's death, and gave him of the best of all that he had, and entertained him for a long time as his guest. But Astydamia, the wife of King Acastus, falsely accused Peleus of another crime, and besought her husband to slay him. Then the heart of Acastus was sad, for he would not shed the blood of one who was his guest. But he persuaded Peleus to join him in hunting wild beasts in the woods of Pelion; for he hoped that then some way might open for him to rid himself of the unfortunate man. All day long they toiled up and down the slopes; they climbed the steep cliffs; they forced their way through brakes and briery thickets; and at last Peleus was so overwearied that he sank down on a bed of moss, and fell asleep. Then Acastus slyly took his weapons from him, and left him there alone and unarmed, hoping that the wild beasts would find and slay him. When Peleus awoke, he saw himself surrounded by mountain robbers; he felt for his sword, but it was gone; even his shield was nowhere to be found. He called aloud to Acastus, but the king was dining at that moment in Iolcos. I heard his cry, however; I knew his voice, and I hastened to his aid. The robbers fled when they saw me coming; and I led my dear but erring grandson back to my cavern, where the days of his boyhood and innocence had been spent.

"But I see that the sun is sinking in the west. I will say no more until after we have partaken of food."

With these words Cheiron arose, and left the room. Odysseus, anxious to become acquainted with the lads, arose also, and walked out into the open air. Achilles was waiting for him just outside the door, and the two boys were soon talking with each other as if they had long been friends.

THE GOLDEN APPLE

AFTER the evening meal had been eaten and the cave-hall set in order, the lads brought armloads of dry sticks and twigs, and threw them upon the fire. And the flame leaped up, and shone upon all around with a ruddy glow; and the great cavern was emptied of gloom, and was so filled with light and warmth that it seemed a fit place for joy and pleasure. Old Cheiron sat upon his high couch like a king upon his throne; and the five comely lads, with Odysseus, sat before him, while Phemius the bard stood leaning against the wall. After Cheiron had played a brief melody upon his harp, and the boys had sung a pleasant song, the wise old master thus began:—

"There is a cavern somewhere on Mount Pelion larger by far and a thousand times more beautiful than this; but its doorway is hidden to mortals, and but few men have ever stood beneath its vaulted roof. In that cavern the ever-living ones who oversee the affairs of men, once held high carnival; for they had met there at the marriage-feast of King Peleus, and the woods and rocks of mighty Pelion echoed with the sound of their merry making. But wherefore should the marriage-feast of a mortal be held in such a place and with guests so noble and so great? I will tell you.

"After Peleus had escaped from the plot which King Acastus had laid for him, he dwelt long time with me; for he feared to go down upon the plain lest the men of Iolcos should seize him by order of Acastus, or the folk of Phthia should kill him in revenge for old Eurytion's death. But the days seemed long to him, thus shut out from fellowship with men, and the sun seemed to move slowly in the heavens; and often he would walk around to the other side of the mountain, and sitting upon a great rock, he would gaze for long hours upon the purple waters of the sea. One morning as thus he sat, he saw the sea nymph Thetis come up out of the waves and walk upon the shore beneath him. Fairer than a dream was she,—more beautiful than any picture of nymph or goddess. She was clad in a robe of sea-green silk, woven by the Naiads in their watery grottos; and there was a chaplet of pearls upon her head, and sandals of sparkling silver were upon her feet.

"As Peleus gazed upon this lovely creature, he heard a voice whispering in his ear. It was the voice of Pallas Athené.

" 'Most luckless of mortal men,' she said, 'there is recompense in store for those who repent of their wrong-doing, and who, leaving the paths of error, turn again to the road of virtue. The immortals have seen thy sorrow for the evil deeds of thy youth, and they have looked with pity upon thee in thy misfortunes. And now thy days of exile and of sore punishment are drawing to an end. Behold the silver-footed Thetis, most beautiful of the nymphs of the sea, whom even the immortals have wooed in vain! She has been sent to this shore, to be won and wedded by thee.'

"Peleus looked up to see the speaker of these words, but he beheld only a blue cloud resting above the mountain-top; he turned his eyes downward again, and, to his grief, the silver-footed Thetis had vanished in the waves. All day he sat and waited for her return, but she came not. When darkness began to fall he sought me in my cave-hall, and told me what he had seen and heard; and I taught him how to win the sea-nymph for his bride.

"So when the sun again gilded the crags of Pelion, brave Peleus hid himself among the rocks close by the sea-washed shore, and waited for the coming of the silver-footed lady of the sea. In a little time she rose, beautiful as the star of morning, from the waves. She sat down upon the beach, and dallied with her golden tresses, and sang sweet songs of a happy land in the depths of the sounding sea. Peleus, bearing in mind what I had taught him, arose from his hiding-place, and caught the beauteous creature in his arms. In vain did she struggle to leap into the waves. Seven times she changed her form as he held her: by turns she changed into a fountain of water, into a cloud of mist, into a burning flame, and into a senseless rock. But Peleus held her fast; and she changed then into a tawny lion, and then into a tall tree, and lastly she took her own matchless form again.

"And Peleus held the lovely Thetis by the hand, and they walked long time together upon the beach, while the birds sang among the leafy trees on Pelion's slopes, and the dolphins sported in the sparkling waters at their feet; and Peleus wooed the silver-footed lady, and won her love, and she promised to be his bride. Then the immortals were glad; and they fitted up the great cavern on Mount Pelion for a banquet hall, and made therein a wedding feast, such as was never seen before. The vaulted roof of the cavern was decked with gems which shone like the stars of heaven; a thousand torches, held by lovely mountain nymphs, flamed from the niches in the high walls; and upon the door of polished marble, tables for ten thousand guests were ranged.

"When the wedding-feast was ready, all those who live on high Olympus, and all the immortals who dwell upon the earth, came to rejoice with King Peleus and his matchless bride; and they brought rich presents for the bridegroom, such as were never given to another man. They gave him a suit of armor, rich and fair, a wonder to behold, which lame Hephaestus with rare skill had wrought and fashioned. Poseidon bestowed on him the deathless horses, Balios and Xanthos, and a deftly-wrought chariot with trimmings of gold. And I, one of the least of the guests, gave him an ashen spear which I had cut on Pelion's top, and fashioned with my own hands.

"At the table sat Zeus, the father of gods and men; and his wife, the white-armed Here; and smile-loving Aphrodite; and gray-eyed Pallas Athené; and all the wisest and the fairest of the immortals. The Nereides, nymphs of the sea, danced in honor of Thetis their sister; and the Muses sang their sweetest songs; and silver-bowed Apollo played upon the lyre. The Fates, too, were there: sad Clotho, twirling her spindle; unloving Lachesis, with wrinkled lips ready to speak the fatal word; and pitiless Atropos, holding in her hand the unsparing shears. And around the table passed the youthful and joy-giving Hebe, pouring out rich draughts of nectar for the guests.

"Yet there was one among all the immortals who had not been invited to the wedding; it was Eris, the daughter of War and Hate. Her scowling features, and her hot and hasty manners, were ill-suited to grace a feast where all should be mirth and gladness; yet in her evil heart she planned to be avenged for the slight which had been put upon her. While the merry-making was at its height, and the company were listening to the music from Apollo's lyre, she came unseen into the hall, and threw a golden apple upon the table. No one knew whence the apple came; but on it were written these words, 'FOR THE FAIREST.'

" 'To whom does it belong?' asked Zeus, stroking his brows in sad perplexity.

"The music ceased, and mirth and jollity fled at once from the banquet. The torches, which lit up the scene, flickered and smoked; the lustre of the gems in the vaulted roof was dimmed; dark clouds canopied the great hall: for Discord had taken her place at the table, uninvited and unwelcome though she was.

" 'The apple belongs to me,' said Here, trying to snatch it; 'for I am the queen, and gods and men honor me as having no peer on earth.'

" 'Not so!' cried white-armed Aphrodite. 'With me dwell Love and Joy; and not only do gods and men sing my praises, but all nature rejoices in my presence. The apple is mine, and I will have it!'

"Then Athené joined in the quarrel. 'What is it to be a queen,' said she, 'if at the same time one lacks that good temper which sweetens life? What is it to have a handsome form and face, while the mind is uncouth and ill-looking? Beauty of mind is better than beauty of face; for the former is immortal, while the latter fades and dies. Hence no one has a better right than I to be called the fairest.'

"Then the strife spread among the guests in the hall, each taking sides with the goddess that he loved best; and, where peace and merriment had reigned, now hot words and bitter wrangling were heard. And had not Zeus bidden them keep silence, thus putting an end to the quarrel, all Pelion would have been rent, and the earth shaken to its centre by the mêlée that would have followed.

" 'Let us waste no words over this matter,' he said. 'It is not for the immortals to say who of their number is most beautiful. But on the slopes of Mount Ida, far across the sea, the fairest of the sons of men—Paris, the son of Trojan Priam—keeps his flocks; let him judge who is fairest, and let the apple be hers to whom he gives it.'

"Then Hermes, the swift-footed messenger, arose, and led the three goddesses over sea and land to distant Ida, where Paris, with no thought of the wonderful life which lay before him, piped on his shepherd's reeds, and tended his flock of sheep."

Here Cheiron paused in his story; and the five lads, who had heard it oftentimes before, bade him a kind good-night, and withdrew into an inner chamber to pass the hours in sleep. When more wood had been thrown upon the fire, and the flames leaped up high and bright towards the roof of the cave, Odysseus and Phemius sat down again before the wise old master, and asked him to finish the tale which he had begun.

"But first tell us," said Odysseus, "about that Paris, who was to award the golden apple to the one whom he should deem the fairest."

Then Cheiron smiled, and went on thus with his story:—

"On the other side of the sea there stands a city, rich and mighty, the like of which there is none in Hellas. There an old man, named Priam, rules over a happy and peace-loving people. He dwells in a great palace of polished marble, on a hill overlooking the plain; and his granaries are stored with corn, and his flocks and herds are pastured on the hills and mountain slopes behind the city. Many sons has King Priam; and they are brave and noble youths, well worthy of such a father. The eldest of these sons is Hector, who, the Trojans hope, will live to bring great honor to his native land. Just before the second son was born, a strange thing troubled the family of old Priam. The queen had dreamed that her babe had turned into a firebrand, which burned up the walls and the high towers of Troy, and left but smouldering ashes where once the proud city stood. She told the king her dream; and when the child was born, they called a soothsayer, who could foresee the mysteries of the future, and they asked him what the vision meant.

" 'It means,' said he, 'that this babe, if he lives, shall be a firebrand in Troy, and shall turn its walls and its high towers into heaps of smouldering ashes.'

" 'But what shall be done with the child, that he may not do this terrible thing?' asked Priam, greatly sorrowing, for the babe was very beautiful.

" 'Do not suffer that he shall live,' answered the soothsayer.

"But Priam, the gentlest and most kind-hearted of men, could not bear to harm the babe. So he called Archelaus, his master shepherd, and bade him take the helpless child into the thick woods, which grow high up on the slopes of Ida, and there to leave him alone. The wild beasts that roam among those woods, he thought, would doubtless find him, or, in any case, he could not live long without care and nourishment; and thus the dangerous brand would be quenched while yet it was scarcely a spark.

"The shepherd did as he was bidden, although it cost his heart many a sharp pang thus to deal barbarously with the innocent. He laid the smiling infant, wrapped in its broidered tunic, close by the foot of an oak, and then hurried away that he might not hear its cries. But the Dryads, who haunt the woods and groves, saw the babe, and pitied its helplessness, and cared for it so that it did not die. Some brought it yellow honey from the stores of the wild bees; some fed it with milk from the white goats that pastured on the mountain side; and others stood as sentinels around it, guarding it from the wolves and bears. Thus five days passed, and Archelaus the shepherd, who could not forget the babe, came cautiously to the spot to see if, mayhap, even its broidered cloak had been spared by the beasts. Sorrowful and shuddering he glanced toward the foot of the tree. To his surprise, the babe was still there; it looked up and smiled, and stretched its fat hands toward him. The shepherd's heart would not let him turn away the second time. He took the child in his arms, and carried it to his own humble home in the valley, where he cared for it and brought it up as his own son.

"The boy grew to be very tall and very handsome; and he was so brave, and so helpful to the shepherds around Mount Ida, that they called him Alexandros, or the helper of men; but his foster-father named him Paris. And as he tended his sheep in the mountain dells, he met Œnone, the fairest of the river-maidens, guileless and pure as the waters of the stream by whose banks she loved to wander. Day after day he sat with her in the shadow of her woodland home, and talked of innocence and beauty, and of a life of sweet contentment, and of love; and the maiden listened to him with wide-open eyes and a heart full of trustfulness and faith. Then, by and by, Paris and Œnone were wedded; and their little cottage in the mountain glen was the fairest and happiest spot in Ilios. The days sped swiftly by, and neither of them dreamed that any sorrow was in store for them; and to Œnone her shepherd-husband was all the world, because he was so noble and brave and handsome and gentle.

"One warm summer afternoon, Paris sat in the shade of a tree at the foot of Mount Ida, while his flocks were pasturing upon the hillside before him. The bees were humming lazily among the flowers; the cicadas were chirping among the leaves above his head; and now and then a bird twittered softly among the bushes behind him. All else was still, as if enjoying to the full the delicious calm of that pleasant day. Paris was fashioning a slender reed into a shepherd's flute; while Œnone, sitting in the deeper shadows of some clustering vines, was busy with some simple piece of needlework. A sound as of sweet music caused the young shepherd to raise his eyes. Before him stood the four immortals, Here, Athené, Aphrodite, and Hermes the messenger; their faces shone with a dazzling radiance, and they were fairer than any tongue can describe. At their feet rare flowers sprang up, crocuses and asphodels and white lilies; and the air was filled with the odor of orange blossoms. Paris, scarce knowing what he did, arose to greet them. No handsomer youth ever stood in the presence of beauty. Straight as a mountain pine was he; a leopard skin hung carelessly upon his shoulders; his head was bare, but his locks clustered round his temples in sunny curls, and formed fit framework for his fair brows.

"Then Hermes spoke first: 'Paris, we have come to seek thy help; there is strife among the folk who dwell on Mount Olympus. Here are Here, Athené, and Aphrodite, each claiming to be the fairest, and each clamoring for this prize, this golden apple. Now we pray that you will judge this matter, and give the apple to the one whom you may deem most beautiful.'

"Then Here began her plea at once: 'I know that I am the fairest,' she said, 'for I am queen, and mine it is to rule among gods and men. Give me the prize, and you shall have wealth, and a kingdom, and great glory; and men in after-times shall sing your praises.'

"And Paris was half tempted to give the apple, without further ado, to Here the proud queen. But gray-eyed Athené spoke: 'There is that, fair youth, which is better than riches or honor or great glory. Listen to me, and I will give thee wisdom and a pure heart; and thy life shall be crowned with peace, and sweetened with love, and made strong by knowledge. And though men may not sing of thee in after-times, thou shalt find lasting happiness in the answer of a good conscience towards all things.'

"Then Œnone whispered from her place among the leaves, 'Give the prize to Athené; she is the fairest.' And Paris would have placed the golden apple in her hand, had not Aphrodite stepped quickly forward, and in the sweetest, merriest tones, addressed him.

" 'You may look at my face, and judge for yourself as to whether I am fair,' said she, laughing, and tossing her curls. 'All I shall say is this: Give me the prize, and you shall have for your wife the most beautiful woman in the world.'

"The heart of Œnone stood still as Paris placed the apple in Aphrodite's hand; and a nameless dread came over her, as if the earth were sinking beneath her feet. But the next moment the blood came back to her cheeks, and she breathed free and strong again; for she heard Paris say, 'I have a wife, Œnone, who to me is the loveliest of mortals, and I care not for your offer; yet I give to you the apple, for I know that you are the fairest among the deathless ones who live on high Olympus.'

"On the very next day it happened that King Priam sat thoughtfully in his palace, and all his boys and girls—nearly fifty in number—were about him.

His mind turned sadly to the little babe whom he had sent away, many years ago, to die alone on wooded Ida. And he said to himself, 'The child has been long dead, and yet no feast has been given to the gods that they may make his little spirit glad in the shadowy land of Hades. This must not be neglected longer. Within three days a feast must be made, and we will hold games in his honor.'

"Then he called his servants, and bade them go to the pastures on Mount Ida, and choose from the herds that were there the fattest and handsomest bull, to be given as a prize to the winner in the games. And he proclaimed through all Ilios, that on the third day there would be a great feast in Troy, and games would be held in honor of the little babe who had died twenty years before. Now, when the servants came to Mount Ida, they chose a bull for which Paris had long cared, and which he loved more than any other. And he would not let the beast be driven from the pasture until it was agreed that he might go to the city with it and contend in the games for the prize. But Œnone, the river-nymph, wept and prayed him not to go.

" 'Leave not the pleasant pasture lands of Ida, even for a day,' said she; 'for my heart tells me that you will not return.'

" 'Think not so, my fair one,' said Paris. 'Did not Aphrodite promise that the most beautiful woman in the world shall be my wife? And who is more beautiful than my own Œnone? Dry now your tears; for when I have won the prizes in the games I will come back to you, and never leave you again.'

"Then the grief of Œnone waxed still greater. 'If you will go,' she cried, 'then hear my warning! Long years shall pass ere you shall come again to wooded Ida, and the hearts which now are young shall grow old and feeble by reason of much sorrow. Cruel war and many dire disasters shall overtake you, and death shall be nigh unto you; and then Œnone, although long forgotten by you, will hasten to your side, to help and to heal and to forgive, that so the old love may live again. Farewell!'

"But Paris kissed his wife, and hastened, light of heart, to Troy. How could it be otherwise but that, in the games which followed, the handsome young shepherd should carry off all the prizes?

" 'Who are you?' asked the king.

" 'My name is Paris,' answered the shepherd, 'and I feed the flocks and herds on wooded Ida.'

"Then Hector, full of wrath because of his own failure to win a prize, came forward to dispute with Paris.

" 'Stand there, Hector,' cried old Priam; 'stand close to the young shepherd, and let us look at you!' Then turning to the queen, he asked, 'Did you ever see two so nearly alike? The shepherd is fairer and of slighter build, it is true; but they have the same eye, the same frown, the same smile, the same motion of the shoulders, the same walk. Ah, what if the young babe did not die after all?'

"Then Priam's daughter Cassandra, who has the gift of prophecy, cried out, 'Oh, blind of eye and heart, that you cannot see in this young shepherd the child whom you sent to sleep the sleep of death on Ida's wooded slopes!'

"And so it came about, that Paris was taken into his father's house, and given the place of honor which was his by right. And he forgot Œnone his fair young wife, and left her to pine in loneliness among the woods and in the narrow dells of sunny Ida."

By this time the fire had burned low upon the hearth, and Cheiron the master would fain have ended his talk. But Odysseus was anxious to hear more.

"To-morrow," said he, "we must go back to Iolcos, for perchance the ships of Peleus may then be ready to sail. So tell us, I pray you, yet more about that strange wedding feast in the cavern halls of Pelion."

"There is little more to tell," said the master. "After the feast, King Peleus went down with his bride into Phthia; and there his Myrmidons, who had waited so long for his coming, rallied around him, ready to help him in any undertaking. And they marched upon Iolcos, and entered the gates, carrying all before them; and they slew King Acastus, and set Peleus on his throne. Thus ended this hero's days of exile; and now for seven years he has ruled Iolcos and Phthia both wisely and well; yet, though you have found him at this season of the year in Iolcos, he loves best his old home of Phthia, where dwell his Myrmidons."

"Please tell me about his son, fair young Achilles, who is here in your hall," said Odysseus.

Cheiron answered briefly by telling how the young lad's mother, the sea nymph Thetis, had longed to make her son immortal; and how it was said that she each night threw him into the fire to purge away whatever mortal stains might cling to him; and how each day she anointed him with ambrosia, and sang him to sleep with sweet lullabies of the sea.

"But one night," added Cheiron, "King Peleus happened to see the babe lying in the fire; and in his fright he cried out, and snatched him from the coals. Then Thetis sorrowfully gave up her plan; and the boy was sent to me, that I might train him in all that goes to the making of a man. There are those who say that I feed the lad on the hearts of lions, and the marrow of bears and wild boars; and those may believe the story who wish to do so. But I have lived long enough to know that there are other and better ways of training up heroes, and fitting them for the strife of battle."

And thus the long talk with Cheiron, the wise master, ended; and Odysseus retired to his couch, and was soon dreaming of far-away Ithaca and of his anxious mother, who was even then hoping for his return.

The next morning the lad and his tutor went down the mountain; and, following the pathway which Jason had taken when he went to claim his birthright of Pelias, they came, in good time, back to Iolcos by the sea. There they found that a ship was just making ready to sail for Corinth; and bidding a hasty farewell to King Peleus, and to bold Echion, who still tarried there, they embarked, and were soon well on their way. The voyage was a long and hard one; but kind Athené favored them, and Poseidon gave them smooth waters and many pleasant days upon the sea. Nor were they delayed at Corinth; for they found waiting there a ship, which Laertes had sent out on purpose to meet them and bring them home. And so, before the autumn had closed, Odysseus, much wiser and stronger than he was when he departed, gazed with glad eyes once more upon the shores of sea-girt Ithaca.

ADVENTURE IX

THE SWINEHERD

WHEN Odysseus stepped ashore upon the sandy beach of Ithaca, the good people of the town, both young and old, had gathered there to welcome him; and they sang a song of greeting like that with which they were wont to meet their returning heroes. He staid only a moment to speak with them. With winged feet he hastened to the hall where his queenly mother waited for his coming. She threw her arms about him, and in the fulness of her joy wept aloud; and she kissed his head and his eyes and both his hands, and welcomed him as one saved from death.

"Thou hast come at last, Odysseus," she said. "The light is not more sweet to me. I feared that I should never see thee more, when I heard that thou hadst gone from Parnassus to distant Pelion. Come now, and sit before me as of yore, and let me look into those eyes which have been so long time away."

And Laertes, too, folded the boy in his arms, and kissed him, and plied him with a thousand questions which he could not answer. Then, in the halls of the king, a feast was made ready, and the day was given over to music and merry-making; and all the people joined in offering thanks to Pallas Athené, who had brought the wanderer safe home to his friends and his kindred.

When the evening had come, and the guests had gone to their own homes, Odysseus sat upon a low stool at his mother's feet; while she asked him many questions about her aged sire Autolycus, and about the dear home of her girlhood on the farther side of Mount Parnassus. And he told her of all that she asked him, and of the wonderful things that he had seen and heard in far-away lands and seas.

"But were you not afraid that evil would befall you, and that your eyes would never more behold fair Ithaca?" asked his mother, tenderly stroking his yellow hair.

"Nightly I prayed to Pallas Athené," answered the lad, "and she watched kindly over me every hour. Who would be afraid when shielded and led by so great a friend? Then, too, good Phemius questioned the Pythian oracle about me; and the answer was such as to make me sure of safety. It was this:—

'To home and kindred he shall safe return ere long,
    With scars well-won, and greeted with triumphal song.' "

"Well," said Laertes, "the oracle doubtless spoke the truth. We know that you have returned to your home, and that you have been greeted with songs, but I fear you have yet to gain the scars."

"Not so, father," answered Odysseus. And then he showed them the great white scar which the tusk of the wild boar had made upon his knee; and he told them of the famous hunt in the woods of Parnassus, and of the days of pain and enforced quiet which he had afterward spent on an invalid's couch. And all those who listened to his story were struck with the wisdom of his thoughts; and they wondered at the choice beauty of the words which fell from his lips, soft and persuasive like the flakes of snow on a quiet day in winter.

After this, many pleasant days came and passed. The simple-hearted folk of Ithaca went about their tasks as of yore,—some tending their flocks in the mountain pastures, some gathering the autumn fruits from the overladen trees, and some twirling the spindle or plying the loom in their humble homes. King Laertes himself worked early and late in his vineyards or in his well-tilled orchard grounds; and Odysseus was often with him, as busy as he, tending his own trees and vines. For, long time before, when he was but a little child, the boy had walked through these grounds with his father, and had asked the names of the trees. And Laertes had not only answered the prattler, but had given him a whole small orchard for his own: of pear trees, thirteen; of apple trees, ten; of fig trees, forty; and he promised to give him fifty rows of vines, each of which ripened at a different time, with all manner of clusters on their boughs.

Sometimes Odysseus went out with other boys of his age to ramble among the hills and on the wooded mountain slopes. Sometimes they played at ball in the open field, or loitered around the flowing spring whence the people of the town drew water. This well had been digged and walled by Ithacus and Neritus, the first settlers of the island; and close by it was a thicket of reeds and alders, growing green and rank from the boggy soil; while, on the rock from beneath which the ice-cold water gushed, an altar had been built, where all wayfarers laid some offering for the nymphs. This was a lovely spot; and in the heat of the day, the boys would often sit in the cool shade of the trees, and play a quiet game with pebbles, or talk about the noble deeds of the heroes.

Once they wandered far over the hills to the sheltered woodland where the swine of Laertes were kept. There, near the rock called Corax, was the spring of Arethusa, around which grew many great oak trees, yielding abundance of acorns. Here the slave Eumæus lived in a humble lodge of his own building, and fed and tended his master's swine, far from the homes of other men.

When the swineherd saw Odysseus, and knew that he was the master's son, he ran to welcome him and his comrades to his lowly home. He led them to the lodge, and took them in, and strewed fragrant leaves upon the floor, and stirred the blazing fire upon the hearth. Then he hastened to the sties where the fattest young pigs were penned. Two of these he killed and dressed; and when he had cut them in pieces, he roasted the choicest parts on spits before the fire. Then he set the smoking food upon a table before Odysseus and his comrades, and sprinkled it all over with white barley-meal. After this, he mixed honey-sweet wine with water in a wooden bowl, and sat down to the feast with them. Right heartily did they eat and drink, and many were the pleasant jests that were passed among them. When they had finished, Odysseus said,—

"Swineherd Eumæus, you have fed us right nobly, and there is nothing more welcome to tired and hungry boys than plenty of well-seasoned food. Surely one who can serve so royally as you have done was not born a slave?"

"Nor indeed was I," answered Eumæus. "In my childhood I was a prince, noble as yourself. But the Fates bring strange fortunes to some men, and strangely have I been tossed about in the world."

"Do tell us," said Odysseus, "how this great change was made in your life. Was the goodly town in which your father and your lady mother dwelt, laid waste by an enemy? Or did unfriendly men find you in the fields alone, and sell you to him who would pay the goodliest price?"

"Since you ask me for my story, young master," said Eumæus, "I will tell it you. But sit you here upon this couch of goat skins while you listen, for I know that your long walk has wearied you.

"Far out in the sea there is an island called Syria, above which the sun turns in its course. It is not very thickly peopled, but it is rich in vineyards and wheatfields, and in pastures where thousands of cattle graze. There no one ever goes hungry for lack of food, and sickness never comes; but when men grow old, then silver-bowed Apollo, and Artemis his huntress sister, strike them with their noiseless arrows, and they cease to live. In that island stand two cities, fair and rich; and over them both my father is sole lord and king. There, in his white halls where care never enters, my infancy was passed; and never did I dream of the hard lot which the pitiless Fates had decreed for me.

"One day there came to our island some Phœnician merchants, shrewd seafaring men, intent on trade and profit. In their ship they brought countless trinkets to barter with our folk for corn and wine; and they moored their vessel in the harbor close to the shore. In my father's house there dwelt a Phœnician slave-woman, tall and fair, and skilled in needlework. And when the merchants knew that she spoke their language, they asked her who she was and from whence she came.

" 'In Sidon I was born,' she answered, 'and Arybas my father was one of the wealthiest of Sidonian merchants. Once as I was walking on the shore, a band of Taphian sea-robbers seized me unawares, and carried me in their dark-hulled ship across the sea. They brought me to this far-distant island, and sold me, for much gold, to the man who lives in yonder palace.' And she pointed to my father's lofty dwelling.

"Then the merchants asked her if she would return with them to Sidon, where she might again behold her father and mother, and the sweet home of her girlhood. And she consented, only asking that they pledge themselves to take her safely home.

" 'Now say no more,' she said; 'and should any of you meet me on the road or by the well, hold your tongues, and let no word be spoken between us. But when you have sold your goods, and have filled your ship with corn and wine, send some one to the house who shall tell me secretly. Then I will hie me to your swift-sailing vessel, bringing gold wherewith to pay my fare, and, if fortune favor, even more than gold. For I am nurse to the little son of my master, a cunning prattler whom I often take with me in my walks. I will bring him on board your ship, and when you have reached some rich foreign land you can sell him for a goodly price.'

"And thus having settled upon a plan, the Phœnician woman went back to my father's halls; and the merchants staid a whole year in our harbor, and filled their ship with grain. But when at last they were ready to sail, they sent a messenger to tell the woman. He came to our house with many trinkets, bracelets, and golden necklaces, which pleased the eyes of my lady mother and her maidens. And while they were looking, and asking the price, he signed to my Phœnician nurse, and straightway gathered up his goods, and hastened back to his fellows. When the sun went down, the woman took my hand, and led me from the house as she had often done before. Thoughtlessly I followed her to the shore where the fast-sailing ship was moored. The Phœnicians took us both on board; they hoisted the broad sail, and a brisk wind quickly carried us far away from my home and friends. On the seventh day, Artemis the archer queen smote the woman with her silent arrows, and her eyes saw no more the sweet light of heaven. Then the crew cast her forth into the sea, to be food for fishes and the sea calves; and I was left alone and stricken with grief and fear. But the swift ship brought us ere long to Ithaca, and there those who had stolen me bartered me to Laertes for a goodly price. And that is why I am your father's thrall, and dwell here lonely underneath these sheltering oaks."

Such was the tale which the swineherd told Odysseus and his young companions as they sat together in the lodge.

"I pity thee, Eumæus," said the lad. "Thy story is indeed a sad one; and, could I do so, I would gladly send thee back to far-off Syria where thy mother sorrows even yet for thee."

"Alas!" answered the swineherd. "There is no hope. No ship will ever sail through the unknown seaways which lead to my boyhood's home. My life must be spent in this spot; yet I am happy in knowing that my master is the kindest of men, and that I shall be well provided for. Even a slave may find enjoyment if his heart be right; for it is the mind, and not the force of outward things, that makes us rich and free."

THE SEA ROBBERS OF MESSENE

FIVE years passed quietly by, and brought few changes to Ithaca. The flocks still grazed in their mountain pastures; the orchard trees still bent under their loads of ripening fruit; the vines still yielded their treasures of purple and red. The simple-hearted islanders arose each day with the coming of the dawn; they went about their tasks with cheerfulness; they sang, and danced, and ate their accustomed meals, and then with the coming of night they lay down to sleep: to them, all days were alike, and life was but one pleasant round of duties. But King Laertes, as he grew older, sought more and more the quiet of his farm and garden; and, for the most part, he allowed his little kingdom to take care of itself, and his subjects to do as they pleased.

And in these five years young Odysseus had become a man. He had grown not so much in stature as in wisdom, nor yet so much in size of limb and body as in strength of bone and muscle. There was nothing in his face or figure that could be called handsome, and yet he was the pride of Ithaca. For, in all the deeds and feats most worthy of men, he was without a peer. In wrestling and leaping, in rowing and swimming, in shooting with the bow, and in handling the heavy spear, there was no one that could equal him. He was a very master of words; and when his speech warmed into earnestness, the dullest hearer was spell-bound by his eloquence. Even to the Achaian mainland and among the islands of the sea, he was famed for his far-reaching shrewdness. Indeed, his craftiness oftentimes outweighed his sense of honor; for, in that early day, to outwit one's fellows even by fraud was thought to be praiseworthy.

One evening in summer, four strange ships, with long black hulls, sailed into the harbor at Ithaca, and were moored in the deep water close to the shore. They were found to be manned by crews of seafarers from the low-lying shores of Messene; and their captain brought greetings from Orsilochus their king, and offered to barter silver and merchandise for Ithacan wool and long-horned sheep. Laertes welcomed the strangers warmly; and as the night was near, he advised that early on the morrow they should bring their wares ashore, and allow his people to bargain for what they needed most. And soon darkness covered all the ways, and Ithaca was wrapped in slumber.

When the gray dawn peeped into his chamber, and awakened him, the king arose, and looked out towards the harbor. Not one of the black-hulled ships could he see. They had silently cast their moorings, and had stolen away through the darkness. While the king looked and wondered, an old shepherd with frightened face and gestures of alarm came running in breathless haste to the palace. In a few words he told what strange things had happened. By the light of the waning moon, the sea rovers from Messene had sailed around to a little cove where the pastures slope down to the water's edge. There they had landed, and without much ado had driven a whole flock of sheep aboard their ships,—three hundred long-wooled ewes and bleating lambs, the choicest of the fields. And they had carried away not only these, but the six sleepy shepherds whose duty it had been to guard them.

An alarm was quickly sounded, and the news was passed from mouth to mouth until it was known to all. The bravest men of Ithaca hastened to the shore, where stood Odysseus and his father, ready to direct them. Their fleetest vessels, lying high upon the beach, were cleared ready to be launched. Five ships with vermilion prows were pushed into the waves; and each was manned by a score of lusty rowers, and headed towards the open sea. The long oars dipped into the water, as if all were moved by a single hand; and the vessels sped out upon their errand, like dogs of the chase intent upon a fleeing victim.

The sky was clear. The waves danced merrily in the sunlight. The wind blew gently from the shore. The crews of the Ithacan ships bent to the oars like practised seamen; but when they rounded the headlands at the foot of the bay, and came out upon the open sea, they saw no trace of the pirate fleet, nor even a single sail upon the laughing face of the deep. Whether the men of Messene had pushed straight homeward with their plunder, or whether they had put into some other cove or inlet farther down the coast, no one could guess. All that their pursuers could do was to sail close along the shore, southward towards Cephallenia, peering behind every jutting headland, and into every sheltered nook, in hopes of coming upon them.

Five days afterward, the red-prowed ships returned to Ithaca. Nothing had been seen of the sea robbers: nothing had been heard of the stolen flocks.

What was to be done? The robbers were known to be men of Messene, the subjects of Orsilochus. It was no secret, that much of the wealth of Messene had been gotten by the plunder and pillage of foreign coasts; but were the pirates of that country to be allowed thus to rob their near neighbors and kinsfolk? Laertes called together a council of the chiefs and elders, and asked them what it was best to do.

"We are a peaceful, home-loving people," said some of the older men, "and it would neither be wise nor pleasant to entangle ourselves in a war with a strong king like Orsilochus. The loss of three hundred sheep is not much where there are so many, and it is not likely that the sea robbers will ever trouble us again. Let us go quietly back to our fields and homes, and leave well enough alone."

But the young men would not listen to a plan so tame and spiritless. They were eager, if they could not recover what was their own, to take at least what was of equal value from the Messenians. It would be easy, they said, for a few stanch ships with well-chosen crews to cross the sea-ways, and land by night upon the rich coast of Messene; there they could fill the roomy holds of their vessels with fruit and grain; and before any one could hinder, they would sail safely back to Ithaca laden with wealth far greater than three hundred sheep.

Then Odysseus, though a mere youth among bearded men, stood up before them, and said,—

"My good friends, I like neither the one plan nor the other. It is but the part of a slave to suffer wrong without striking back. It is but the part of a coward to strike in the dark, as if fearing the enemy's face. Why not send boldly to Messene, and demand either the stolen sheep, or a fair price for them? I myself will undertake the business, and I promise you that I will bring back to Ithaca gifts and goods worth twice as much as the flock that has been taken."

The elders listened with favor to the young man's words; and, after further talk, it was settled that he should go forthwith across the sea to claim the debt which was due from the people of Messene.

The goodliest ship of all the Ithacan galleys was made ready for Odysseus. The needed stores of food and drink were brought on board, and placed in the vessel's hold. The young hero, with his friend and tutor Phemius, climbed over the vessel's side, and sat down in the prow. The long-haired seamen cast loose the moorings; they plied their oars, and the swift ship was soon far out upon the waters. A steady north wind filled the sail, and the vessel sped swiftly on her way, cleaving the white foam with her keel. By and by the sun went down, and night wrapped the world in her sober mantle, but the ship still held its course, being guided by the moon's pale light, and the steadfast star of the north.

The next day they sailed within sight of the low-lying coast of Elis, which stretched northward and southward farther than their eyes could reach. Yet they turned not to the shore, but sailed straight on; for Odysseus, advised by Pallas Athené, wished first to visit Pylos, where wise old Nestor ruled with his father, the ancient Neleus. This Neleus was the uncle of Jason, chief of the Argonauts, and had been driven from Iolcos by Pelias the usurper. Long time had he wandered, an exile in strange lands, until Aphareus of Arene gave him leave to build a city on the sandy plain close by the sea. There he had reared a noble palace; and there he still dwelt, having outlived three generations of men. But he had given up his kingdom, many years before, to his son Nestor, himself a sage old man.

It was not until late on the third day that the voyagers turned their ship's prow into the harbor of Pylos. It touched the shore, and Odysseus with his tutor sprang out upon the sands. They found the people of the city offering sacrifices there to Poseidon, ruler of the deep. Upon nine long seats they were sitting, five hundred or more on each seat; and the priest stood up before them, pouring out libations and offering sacrifices. Nine coal-black heifers he offered to Poseidon.

King Nestor sat upon a lofty seat while the elders of the city stood around him, or plied their several duties at the feast. Some of them were busy cutting choice bits of flesh from the slaughtered beeves; others fixed these bits upon spits, and roasted them over heaps of glowing coals; and still others handed the smoking food to the waiting people who sat hungry in their places. When Nestor saw Odysseus and the bard, two strangers, standing upon the shore, he arose and went down to meet them. He gave to each a hand, and leading them to the feast he seated them upon soft skins spread on piles of yielding sand. Then he brought to them, in his own hands, choicest pieces of well-cooked and well-flavored food; and when they had eaten as much as they liked, he poured rich wine into a golden goblet, and as he offered it first to the noble bard he said, "Right welcome are you, stranger, whoever you may be, to this our midsummer festival. I give this golden goblet to you first, you being the older man, that you may pray as beseemeth you to great Poseidon. When you have made your prayer, hand then the cup to the young man who is with you, that he too may pour out a libation; for all men have need to pray."

Then the bard took the goblet, and pouring out a rich libation, lifted up his eyes and prayed, "Great Poseidon, thou who dost hold the earth in thy strong arms, hear now the prayer of thy suppliant. Prolong still the life of our aged host, and add to Nestor with each circling year new honors and greater wealth. To the folk of Pylos give rich contentment and that peace which is the befitting prize of those who are mindful of life's varied duties. And lastly, grant that this young man may find that which he seeks, and then return rejoicing to his home and friends."

When he had thus spoken, he gave the goblet to Odysseus, and he in like manner poured out libations, and prayed to great Poseidon.

Then said Nestor as he took again the goblet, "Strangers, you do wisely thus to offer prayers to the gods; for they are far above us in virtue, strength, and honor. When men have failed to do aright, and have broken Heaven's just laws, they may still, by humble vows and supplications, turn aside from evil-doing, and soften the wrath of the ever-living powers."

"Yes, truly," answered Phemius, "by prayers we do honor both ourselves and those to whom we pray. There is an ancient saying, which no doubt you oft have heard, that prayers are the feeble-sighted daughters of Father Zeus, and wrinkled and lame they follow in misfortune's track. But misfortune, strong and swift, outruns them often, and brings distress upon the sons of men; then these blessed prayers, following after, kindly heal the hurts and bind up the aching wounds which have been made. And for this reason the man who is wont to pray feels less the strokes of fortune than does he who lives forgetful of the gods."

The feast being soon ended, Nestor turned again to the strangers, and said, "Behold now, the day is well-nigh gone, and all have paid their vows to the ever-living gods. The time has come when we may ask our stranger-guests their names and errand. Who are you who come thus unheralded to the sandy shores of Pylos? Is your visit one of peace, and shall we welcome you as friends? Or do you come as spies, to find out what there may be of wealth or of weakness in our city?"

Odysseus answered: "O noble Nestor, we will speak the truth, and hide nothing from you. I am Odysseus of Ithaca; my father is King Laertes, who was once your comrade when you sailed on the Argo to golden Colchis. Ten days ago, there came to our island sea-faring men from Messene, whom we welcomed as friends and neighbors. But under cover of the night they landed on our shores; they seized three hundred of our long-wooled sheep, together with the shepherds, and bore them across the sea to some one of the pirate harbors of Messene. I now am on my way to King Orsilochus, to bid him send back the stolen flock; and if he will not hearken to my words, then I shall either gain by guile or take by force double the value of the sheep. But I have come first to Pylos, that you, my father's old-time friend, might know my errand, and, if need be, lend me your aid."

"You have spoken well," answered Nestor; "and for your father's sake you are thrice welcome to the lofty halls of Pylos. Abide with me for one night, and in the morning I will give you a car and steeds, and a trustworthy guide, to take you by the straightest road to Pherae, where the king of Messene dwells. Orsilochus must learn from me, that, though his pirate-crews may plunder foreign shores, they must not molest the flocks and goods of our home-staying neighbors."

Having thus spoken, he led the way to the fair palace, which his father Neleus erstwhile had built. There they found that aged chieftain sitting in the great hall, upon a soft couch spread with purple coverings. His hair and his long beard were white as the driven snow, and his hands trembled from very feebleness, for he was exceeding old. He spoke kindly to Odysseus, and asked many questions about his father Laertes, and his home in Ithaca; but he seemed most pleased when the young man told him of his visit, when a boy, to Iolcos and Mount Pelion. For Iolcos had been the home of Neleus in his youth; and he it was who had helped Pelias drive Æson from the kingdom which was his by right. But Nemesis had followed him, and punished him for the deed.

Soon the shades of night began to darken the fair hall, and the chiefs and elders went each one to his own house. But Nestor led Odysseus and the bard to an upper chamber, where a fair, soft couch was spread upon a jointed bedstead. There he left them for the night, and there they soon found rest in soothing slumber.

As soon as the light of day began to streak the eastern sky, the aged Neleus, as was his wont, arose from his couch, and, leaning on the arm of Nestor, went feebly out, and took his seat upon a smooth white stone before the palace gate. Then every one who had aught of grievance, or had suffered any wrong, came and told his story, and made his plea; and the old hero weighed the matter with an even hand, and gave judgment for the right.

"What shall be done to aid the son of Laertes, that so his journey into Messene shall prosper?" asked Nestor. "Thou knowest that King Orsilochus has ever been our friend and ally; yet shall we allow his lawless men thus to despoil our neighbors and old-time comrades?"

"Send to Pherae, with the young man, a trusty messenger who shall speak for him," answered old Neleus. "Send them both in thy own chariot, and ask Orsilochus, in the name of a friend, to deal justly with the son of Laertes."

By this time Odysseus and the bard had awakened from their slumber. They arose; and when they had bathed, and had been anointed with soft oil, they clothed themselves in robes of noble texture, and went down into the banquet hall. There they found King Nestor waiting; and they sat down with him at the table, and willing servants waited on them, bringing choice food and pouring sweet wine into golden goblets.

When the meal was finished, the bard bade his host farewell; and, praying that the gods would speed Odysseus on his errand, he went down to the red-prowed ship which was waiting by the shore. And as soon as he stepped on board, the sailors loosed the moorings, and set the sail; and a brisk wind bore them swiftly back towards Ithaca.

But Nestor spoke to the young men about him, "Bring out my finest horses, and yoke them forthwith to my lightest car. They shall carry Odysseus on his journey across the plain to Pherae; and my son Antilochus shall bear him company, and be my messenger to the Messenian king."

Soon the car was ready. The young men took their places; and Antilochus touching the restive horses with his whip, they sped across the dusty plain. It was a rough and tiresome journey, along unbroken ways, and roads scarcely marked with tracks of wheels or horses' hoofs; and night had begun to fall ere they came to the river Nedon and the high walls of Pherae where dwelt Orsilochus, the king of Messene.

THE BOW OF EURYTUS

IN Arcadia there is a little mountain stream called Alpheus. It flows through woods and meadows and among the hills for many miles, and then it sinks beneath the rocks. Farther down the valley it rises again, and dancing and sparkling, as if in happy chase of something, it hurries onward towards the plain; but soon it hides itself a second time in underground caverns, making its way through rocky tunnels where the light of day has never been. Then at last it gushes once more from its prison chambers; and, flowing thence with many windings through the fields of Elis, it empties its waters into the sea.

Of this strange river a strange tale is told, and this is what Antilochus related to Odysseus as they rode across the plain towards Pherae:—

"Years ago there was no river Alpheus; the channel through which it flows had not then been hollowed out, and rank grass and tall bending reeds grew thick where now its waters sparkle brightest. It was then that a huntsman, bearing the name of Alpheus, ranged through the woods, and chased the wild deer among the glades and glens of sweet Arcadia. Far away by the lonely sea dwelt Telegona, his fair young wife, and his lovely babe Orsilochus; but dearer than home or wife or babe to Alpheus, was the free life of the huntsman among the mountain solitudes. For he loved the woods and the blue sky and the singing birds, and the frail flowers upon the hillside; and he longed to live among them always, where his ears could listen to their music, and his eyes look upon their beauty.

" 'O Artemis, huntress-queen!' he cried, 'I ask but one boon of thee. Let me ramble forever among these happy scenes!'

"And Artemis heard him, and answered his prayer. For, as he spoke, a bright vision passed before him. A sweet-faced maiden went tripping down the valley, culling the choicest flowers, and singing of hope and joy and the blessedness of a life pure and true. It was Arethusa, the Arcadian nymph, by some supposed to be a daughter of old Nereus, the elder of the sea. Then Alpheus heard no more the songs of the birds, or the music of the breeze; he saw no longer the blue sky above him, or the nodding flowers at his feet: he was blind and deaf to all the world, save only the beautiful nymph. Arethusa was the world to him. He reached out his arms to catch her; but, swifter than a frightened deer, she fled down the valley, through deep ravines and grassy glades and rocky caverns underneath the hills, and out into the grassy meadows, and across the plains of Elis, to the sounding sea. And Alpheus followed, forgetful of every thing but the fleeing vision. When, at length, he reached the sea, he looked back; and, lo! he was no longer a huntsman, but a river doomed to meander forever among the scenes, for love of which he had forgotten his wife and his babe and the duties of life. It was thus that Artemis answered his prayer.

"And men say that Arethusa the nymph was afterwards changed into a fountain; and that to this day, in the far-off island of Ortygia, that fountain gushes from the rocks in an unfailing, crystal stream. But Orsilochus, the babe forgotten by his father, grew to manhood, and in course of time became the king of Pherae and the seafaring people of Messene."

When Odysseus and his companion reached Pherae, the sun had set, and the gates of the palace were closed. But the porter sent a messenger into the hall where King Orsilochus was sitting at the evening meal, who said, "O king, the car of Nestor, our worthy neighbor, stands outside the gate; and in the car are two young men, richly clothed like princes, and bearing themselves in a most princely manner."

Forthwith the king arose, and went out to the gate, and welcomed the young men to his city and his high-built halls. And he took them by the hand,

and led them into the feast-chamber where the chiefs of Pherae and Messene already sat at meat. He put the spears which they bore, in a spear-stand, where were other goodly weapons leaning against the wall. Then he seated them on chairs of cunning workmanship, beneath which were linen rugs of many colors; and he gave to each an oaken footstool for his feet. Then a maid poured water into a basin of silver, that they might wash their hands; and she drew a polished table near them, on which another maid placed white loaves of bread, and many dainties well-pleasing to the taste of tired travellers. And the carver brought divers tempting dishes of roasted meats; and a herald poured red wine into golden bowls, and set them within easy reach.

When they had eaten, and had forgotten their hunger and thirst and weariness, an old blind bard came into the hall; and as he sat in a high seat leaning against a pillar, he took his harp in his hand, and, touching it with his deft fingers, sang sweet songs of the gods and the heroes and famous men. Not until he had finished his music and laid aside his harp, did Orsilochus venture to speak of any thing that might disturb the pleasure of his guests. Then with well-chosen words, he asked them their names and their errand.

"Our fathers," answered Odysseus, "are Nestor and Laertes, well known among the heroes who sailed with Jason to the golden strand of Colchis; and the errand upon which we come is one of right and justice."

And then he told the king how the crews of the Messenian ships had landed in Ithaca, and carried away his father's choicest flock. Orsilochus listened kindly; and when Odysseus had ended, he said, "Think no more of this troublesome matter, for I will see that it is righted at once. The men who dared thus to wrong your father shall restore fourfold the value of the stolen flocks, and shall humbly beg the pardon of Laertes, as well as of myself. I have spoken, and it shall be done; but you must tarry a while with me in Pherae, and be my honored guest."

Thus Odysseus brought to a happy end the quest upon which he had come to Messene and the high-walled town of Pherae. And he tarried many days in the pleasant halls of the king, and was held in higher honor than all the other guests. But Antilochus, on the second morning, mounted again his father's chariot, and journeyed onward into Laconia: why he went thither, and did not return to Pylos, Odysseus was soon to learn.

One evening there came to Pherae a lordly stranger, bringing with him a train of well-armed men and bearing a handsome present for Orsilochus. He was very tall and handsome; he stood erect as a mountain pine, his eyes flashed keen and sharp as those of an eagle; but his long white hair and frosted beard betokened a man of many years, and his furrowed brow showed plainly that he had not lived free from care.

"I am Iphitus of Œchalia," he said, "and I am journeying to Lacedæmon where great Tyndareus rules."

When Odysseus heard the name of Iphitus, he remembered it as that of a dear friend of whom his father had often spoken; and he asked,—

"Are you that Iphitus who sailed with Jason to golden Colchis? And do you remember among your comrades, one Laertes of Ithaca?"

"There is but one Iphitus," was the answer, "and I am he. Never can I forget the noble-hearted Laertes of Ithaca; for, on board the Argo, he was my messmate, my bedfellow, my friend, my sworn brother. There is no man whom I love more dearly. Would that I could see him, or even know that he still lives!"

When he learned that Odysseus was the son of his old-time friend, he was overjoyed; and he took him by the hand, and wept for very gladness. Then he asked the young man a thousand questions about his father and his mother, and his father's little kingdom of Ithaca. And Odysseus answered him truly; for his heart was filled with love for the noble old hero, and he felt justly proud of his friendship. And after this, so long as they staid at Pherae, the young man and the old were constantly together.

One day, as they were walking alone outside of the city walls, Iphitus said, "Do you see this noble bow which I carry, and which I always keep within easy reach?"

"It would be hard not to see it," answered Odysseus, smiling; "for where you are, there also is the bow. I have often wondered why you guard it with so great care."

"It is the bow of my father Eurytus," answered the hero, "and, next to Apollo's silver weapon, it is the most wonderful ever made. My father dwelt in Œchalia, and was skilled in archery above all other men; and the sons of the heroes came to him to learn how to shoot the silent arrow with most deadly aim. Even Heracles, the mightiest of earth-dwellers, was taught by him; but Heracles requited him unkindly.

"In my father's halls, close by the shore of the eastern sea, there were many bright treasures and precious gems and rarest works of art. But more beautiful than any of these, and more precious to my father's heart than any glittering jewel, was our only sister, the lovely Iole. And when Heracles went out from the land of his birth to toil and do the bidding of false Eurystheus, he tarried for a day in my father's halls. There he saw Iole, the blue-eyed maiden, and his great strong heart was taken captive by her gentle will; but the stern words of Eurystheus fell upon his ears, and bade him go forth at once to the labors which had been allotted him. He went; for he had vowed, long time before, always to obey the calls of duty. And Iole grieved for him in secret; yet every day she grew wiser and more beautiful, and every day the tendrils of her love were twined more and more closely about my father's heart.

"Heracles went out to do the thankless tasks which his master Eurystheus had bidden him do. In the swamps of Lerna, he slew the nine-headed Hydra, and dipped his arrows in its poisonous blood. In the forests of Arcadia, he caught the brazen-footed stag sacred to Artemis. In the snowy glens of Erymanthus, he hunted the fierce wild boar which had long been the terror of men; and, having caught him in a net, he carried him to Mycenæ. In Elis he cleansed the stables of Augeas, turning the waters of the river Alpheus into the stalls of his oxen. In the marshes of Stymphalus, he put to flight the loathsome Harpies, and rested not from following them until they were outside the borders of Hellas. In the sunset land of the Hesperides, he plucked the golden apples which hung ripe in the gardens of Here; and he slew the fiery dragon that kept watch and ward around them. And, lastly, he went down into the dark kingdom of Hades, and brought thence the mighty hound Cerberus, carrying him in his strong arms into the very presence of Eurystheus. All these deeds, and many more, did Heracles, because they were tasks set for him by his master; but other things, even mightier than they, did he do because of his love for suffering men. At length, when the days of his servitude to Eurystheus were ended, he came again to Hellas, and dwelt a long time in Calydon with his old-time friend Oineus."

When Iphitus had thus spoken, he was silent for a time; and Odysseus, seeing that he was busy with his own thoughts, asked him no questions. Then, as if talking in a dream he said,—

"Do you see this bow,—the bow of my father Eurytus? Much grief has it brought upon our house; and yet it was not the bow, but my father's overweening pride, that wrought the mischief, and caused me to go sorrowing through life. Shall I finish my story by telling you how it all ended?"

"Tell me all," answered Odysseus.

"My father Eurytus, as I have said, was the king of archers; for no man could draw an arrow with so unerring aim as he, and no man could send it straight to the mark with a more deadly force. Every thought of his waking hours was upon his bow, and he aspired to excel even the archery of Artemis and Apollo. At length he sent a challenge into every city of Hellas: *Whosoever will excel Eurytus in shooting with the bow and arrows, let him come to Œchalia, and try his skill. The prize to be given to him who succeeds is Iole, the fair daughter of Eurytus.'*

"Then there came to the contest, great numbers of young men, the pride of Hellas. But when they saw this wonderful bow of Eurytus, and tried its strength, their hearts sank within them; and when they aimed their shafts at the target, they shot far wide of the mark, and my father sent them home ashamed and without the prize.

" 'My dearest Iole,' he would often say, 'I am not afraid of losing you, for there lives no man who knows the bow as well as I.'

141

"But by and by great Heracles heard of my father's boasts, and of the prize which he had offered.

" 'I will go down to Œchalia,' said he, 'and I will win the fair Iole for my bride.'

"And when he came, my father remembered how he had taught him archery in his youth; and he felt that in his old pupil he had at last found a peer. Yet he would not cease his boasting. 'If the silver-bowed Apollo should come to try his skill, I would not fear to contend even with him.'

"Then the target was set up, so far away that it seemed as if one might as well shoot at the sun.

" 'Now, my good bow,' said my father, 'thou hast never failed me: do thou serve me better to-day than ever before!'

"He drew the strong cord back, bending the bow to its utmost tension; and then the swift arrow leaped from its place, and sped like a beam of light straight towards the mark. But, before it reached its goal, the strength which my father's arm had imparted to it began to fail; it wavered in the air, its point turned downward, and it struck the ground at the foot of the target.

"Then Heracles took up his bow, and carelessly aimed a shaft at the distant mark. Like the lightning which Zeus hurls from the high clouds straight down upon the head of some lordly oak, so flashed the unfailing arrow through the intervening space, piercing the very centre of the target.

" 'Lo, now, Eurytus, my old-time friend,' said Heracles, 'thou seest that I have won the victory over thee. Where now is the prize, even the lovely Iole, that was promised to him who could shoot better than thou?'

"But my father's heart sank within him, and shame and grief took mighty hold of him. And he sent Iole away in a swift-sailing ship, to the farther shores of the sea, and would not give her to Heracles as he had promised. Then the great hero turned him about in anger, and went back to his home in Calydon, threatening vengeance upon the house of Eurytus. I besought my father that he would remember his word, and would call Iole home again, and would send her to Heracles to be his bride. But he would not hearken, for the great sorrow which weighed upon him. He placed his matchless bow in my hands, and bade me keep it until I should find a young hero worthy to bear it.

" 'It has served me well,' he said, 'but I shall never need it more.' Then he bowed his head upon his hands, and when I looked again the life had gone from him. Some men say that Apollo, to punish him for his boasting, slew him with one of his silent arrows; others say that Heracles smote him because he refused to give to the victor the promised prize, even fair Iole, the idol of his heart. But I know that it was grief and shame, and neither Apollo nor Heracles, that brought death upon him.

"As to Heracles, he dwelt a long time in Calydon, where he wooed and won the princess

Deianeira, the daughter of old Oineus; but the memory of Iole, as she had been to him in the bright days of his youth, was never blotted from his mind. And the people of Calydon loved him, because, with all his greatness and his strength, he was the friend and helper of the weak and needy. But one day, at a feast, he killed by accident a little boy in the palace of Oineus, named Eunomos; and his heart was filled with grief, and he took his wife Deianeira, and, leaving Calydon, he journeyed aimlessly about until he came to Trachis in Thessaly. There he built him a home, but his restless spirit would give him no peace; and so, leaving Deianeira in Trachis, he came back towards Argolis by way of the sea. Three moons ago, I met him in Tiryns. He greeted me as a dear old friend, and kindly offered to help me in the undertaking which I had then on foot; for robbers had driven from my pastures twelve brood mares, the finest in all Hellas, and I was searching for them.

" 'Go you with your men into Messene,' said he, 'for doubtless you will find that which you seek among the lawless men who own Orsilochus as king. If you find them not, come again to Tiryns, and I will aid you in further search, and will have them restored to you, even though Hermes, or great Autolycus, be the thief.'

"So I left him, and came hither to Messene, and to the high-walled towers of Pherae; and thus you know my errand which I have kept hidden from Orsilochus. I have found no traces of the stolen

144

mares; and so to-morrow I shall return to Argolis and Tiryns where the great hero waits for me."

Much more would godlike Iphitus have spoken; but now the sun had set, and the two friends hastened back to the palace of Orsilochus.

"Never have I met a man whose friendship I prized more highly than thine," said Odysseus, as they crossed the courtyard, and each was about to retire to his chamber. "I pray that thou wilt take this sharp sword, which was my father's, and this mighty spear, as tokens of the beginnings of a loving friendship." And the young man put the noble weapons into the old hero's hands.

"And do thou take in return an equal present," said Iphitus. "Here is the matchless bow of Eurytus my father; it shall be thine, and shall be to thee a worthy token of the love which I bear towards thee."

Odysseus took the bow. It was a bow of marvellous beauty, and its strength was so great that no man, save its proud new owner, could string it. It was indeed a matchless gift, and a treasure to be prized.

ADVENTURE XII

THE MOST BEAUTIFUL WOMAN IN THE WORLD

VERY early on the following day, Iphitus bade Orsilochus farewell, and started on his journey back towards Tiryns; and Odysseus, to the surprise of all, went with him, riding in the same chariot.

"I know that you want to go into Laconia," Iphitus had said. "Why not go now? For I and my brave men will convoy you safely as far as Lacedæmon; and when there, I will commend you to my old comrades, Castor and Polydeuces, who dwell in the palace of their father, King Tyndareus."

And Odysseus had gladly consented; for, although his host had pressed him hard to stay longer, he was very anxious for many reasons to visit Lacedæmon.

For two days the company travelled slowly eastward. They crossed the mountain land which lies between Messene and Laconia, and came to the plain, rich with wheat-fields, which lay beyond. And now the way was easier, and the road led straight towards Lacedæmon.

At noon on the second day, they rested upon the banks of a little stream; and, as the sun was hot, they sat a long time in the pleasant shade of some trees which grew not far from the roadside. Some distance down the valley they caught glimpses of the high towers of the city; and now and then they heard the sound of busy workers within the walls, or the shouts of the toilers in the neighboring fields. A ride of only a few minutes would bring them to the gates of Lacedæmon.

While they were thus waiting and resting, an old minstrel, who had come out of the city, joined them by the roadside, and began to entertain them. At first he played sweetly upon his lyre, and sang songs, new and old, which he thought would be pleasing to his listeners. Then he told them stories of the times, now long past, when yet men lived in peaceful innocence, unbeset with eating cares.

"And now," he said, "since you are about to enter Lacedæmon, and will spend the night within the kingly halls of great Tyndareus, you must needs hear of the beauty and the courage and the wealth for which this city is far famed among all the states of Hellas. The riches of which we boast cannot be measured like gold and precious stones; our wealth lies in the courage and true-heartedness of our men, and in the beauty and devotedness of our women."

And then he told them of the four wonderful children whom King Tyndareus and his wife Leda had reared in the pleasant halls of Lacedæmon,— Castor and Polydeuces, the devoted brothers; and the sisters, proud Clytemnestra, and Helen the beautiful. He told how Castor and Polydeuces were famed among all the heroes of Greece; how they had sailed with Jason on the Argo; how they had hunted the wild boar in the woods of Calydon; and how they had fought under the banner of Peleus when he stormed the town of Iolcos, and drove the false Acastus from his kingdom. He told how Helen, while yet a mere child, had been stolen from her home and her parents, and carried by Theseus of Athens to far-distant Attica; and how her brothers Castor and Polydeuces had rescued her, and brought her back to her loving friends in Lacedæmon. He told how the two brothers excelled in all the arts of war, and in feats of courage and skill; how Castor was renowned at home and abroad as a tamer of horses, and how Polydeuces was without a peer as a boxer and as a skilful wielder of the sword. And he told how the beauty of Helen had brought hosts of suitors from every quarter of the world; and how her father, old Tyndareus, was all the time beset with courtiers, princes, and heroes, the noblest of the earth,—all beseeching him for the hand of the matchless fair one.

No one knows how long the old man would have kept on talking, had not Iphitus bade him cease. "We have heard already, a thousand times, the tales that you tell us," he said. "Waste no more time with vain words which are on the tongue of every news-monger in Argolis; but make haste back to the city, and say to Castor and Polydeuces that Iphitus, who erstwhile was their comrade on the Argo, waits outside the gates of Lacedæmon."

The minstrel bowed, and said, "It is not for me to act the part of a herald for a stranger. But do you send one of your young men into the city, and I will gladly go with him into the broad palace of the king, where he may announce your coming."

Then Iphitus called to one of the young men in his company, and bade him go before them to the palace, to herald their coming; and the old minstrel went with him.

Now when the sun was beginning to sink behind the heights of lofty Taygetes, the company arose from their resting-place by the roadside, and began to move slowly towards the city. At the same time, two horsemen came out through the gate, and rode rapidly up the valley to meet them. Iphitus waved his long-plumed helmet in the air, and shouted aloud. "There they come," he cried,—"the twin heroes! as noble and as handsome, and seemingly as young, as when we sailed together on the Argo."

It seemed but a moment until the horsemen approached and drew rein before them. They were tall and comely youths, exceedingly fair, and so alike that no man could tell which one was Castor or which Polydeuces. Their armor was of gold, and glowed in the light of the setting sun like watch-fires on the mountain-tops. Their steeds were white as snow, with long manes that glimmered and shone like the silvery beams of the moon on a still summer's evening.

"All hail, our old-time comrade!" they cried. "Welcome to the halls of Lacedæmon! We bid you welcome in the name of our aged father, King Tyndareus."

Then they turned, and led the way to the lofty palace gates.

As Odysseus and his aged friend dismounted from their car, a score of ready squires came out to serve them. Some loosed the horses from the yoke, and led them to the stables, and fed them plentifully with oats and white-barley grains; others tilted the car against the wall of the outer court, so that no careless passer-by would run against or injure it; and still others carried the arms of the heroes into the spacious hall, and leaned them with care against the grooved columns.

Then Castor and Polydeuces, the glorious twins, led the heroes into the broad hall of King Tyndareus. Odysseus gazed about him with wondering eyes, for he had never seen so great magnificence. Walls of polished marble ran this way and that from the brazen threshold; the doors were of carved oak inlaid with gold, and the door-posts were of shining silver. Within were seats and sumptuous couches ranged against the wall, from the entrance even to the inner chambers; and upon them were spread light coverings, woven and embroidered by the deft hands of women. And so great was the sheen of brass, of gold and silver, and of precious gems, within this hall, that the light gleamed from floor to ceiling, like the beams of the sun or the round full moon.

The aged king was pleased to see the heroes; for Iphitus and he had been lifelong friends, firm and true, through every turn of fortune. And when he learned the name and parentage of young Odysseus, he took him by the hand, and bade him welcome for the sake of his father, good Laertes.

The first words of greeting having been spoken, Odysseus, still wondering, went down into the polished baths. There, when he had bathed, he clothed himself in princely garments; and he threw a soft, rich cloak about his shoulders, and made himself ready to stand in the presence of beauty, nobility, and courage. Then Polydeuces led him back into the great hall.

But a change had taken place while he was gone. The king was no longer alone. There stood around him, or sat upon couches, all the noblest young heroes of Hellas. The king's son-in-law, tall Agamemnon of Mycenæ, stood behind the throne; and near him was his handsome brother Menelaus. Among all the princes then at Lacedæmon, these two sons of Atreus were accounted worthiest; for not only did they excel in strength and wisdom, but they were heirs to the kingdom of Argolis, and the lordship over men. Next to them stood Ajax the son of Telamon; he was nephew to old King Peleus, who had wedded the sea-nymph in the cave-halls of Mount Pelion; and among the younger heroes there was none who equalled him in bravery.

Reclining on a couch at the king's left hand was another prince of the same name,—Ajax, the son of Oileus. He had come from distant Locris, where he was noted as the swiftest runner and the most skilful spearsman in all Hellas. He was neither so tall nor so handsome as the son of Telamon; but the very glance of his eye, and the curl of his lip, made men admire and love him.

Below him stood Diomede of Tiryns, who, though still a mere youth, was a very lion in war. His father, brave Tydeus, had met his death while fighting with the Thebans; but he had long ago avenged him.

Idomeneus, a prince of Crete, known far and wide for his skill in wielding the spear, was next, a man already past the prime of life. And beyond him in order were other princes: Philoctetes of Melibœa, famous for his archery; Machaon, son of Asclepius, from Œchalia, the home of Iphitus; Antilochus of Pylos, late the companion of Odysseus; Nireus of Syma, famed only for his comeliness; and Menestheus of Athens, who, in the management of men and horses and the ordering of battle, had not a peer on earth.

All these were in the hall of King Tyndareus; and they received Odysseus with words of seeming kindness, although a shade of jealousy was plainly seen upon their faces. While they were speaking, a minstrel entered, and began to play deftly upon his lyre; and, as he played and sung, two dancers sprang upon the floor, and whirled in giddy mazes about the hall. Then from their high-roofed chamber, where the air was full of sweet perfumes, came three women to listen to the music. Helen, like in form to Artemis the huntress-queen, led the rest; and when Odysseus saw her, he remembered no more the golden splendor which had dazzled his eyes when first he stood upon the threshold of the palace, for every thing else paled in the light of Helen's unspeakable beauty. Next to her came Clytemnestra, who, a few years before, had been wedded to Agamemnon of Mycenæ. She was fair, but not beautiful; and the glance which fell from her eye sent a thrill of pain to the heart of the young hero. The two sisters were followed by their cousin, sweet Penelope, who, blushing like the morning, kept her eyes modestly upon the ground, and looked not once towards the company of princely strangers. And, as she stood leaning against a lofty column, Odysseus wondered within himself whether he admired more the glorious beauty of Helen, or the retiring sweetness of Penelope.

ADVENTURE XIII

A RACE FOR A WIFE

DAYS and weeks passed by, and still Odysseus tarried as a guest at the court of King Tyndareus. His friend Iphitus had gone on to Tiryns to meet the hero Heracles, and had left with him his blessing and the bow of Eurytus. But the young princes who had come to Lacedæmon to woo the beautiful Helen remained in the palace, and each had vowed in the secret of his heart that he would not depart until he had won the matchless lady for his bride. Each had offered to the king gifts of countless value,—gold and jewels, fine horses, and well-wrought armor; and each had prayed him that he would himself set the bride-price for his daughter, and bestow her on whom he would, even on the man who pleased him best. But the king, for reasons of his own, would give them no answer.

All this time, Odysseus held himself aloof from the crowd of wooers, and kept his own counsel; and, though all believed that he too was smitten with love for the peerless Helen, yet in his heart the blue-eyed Penelope reigned queen. One day as he sat alone with Tyndareus in his chamber, he saw that the king was sorely troubled; and he began in his own way to find out the cause of his distress.

"Surely, O king!" he said, "you are the happiest of men. For here you have, in Lacedæmon, every thing that can delight the eye, or please the heart. Wherever you may turn, there you see wealth and beauty; and it is all yours, to do with as you like. Your sons are the bravest in the world; your daughters are the fairest; your palace is the most beautiful; your kingdom is the strongest. There is certainly nothing to be wished for that is not already yours."

"And yet," answered Tyndareus, with a sigh, "I am the most miserable of mortals. I would rather be a witless swineherd in the oak forests, living in a hut, and feeding upon roots and wild fruits, than dwell in this palace, beset with cares like those which daily weigh me down."

"I cannot understand you," said Odysseus. "You are at peace with all the world; your children are all with you; you have no lack of comfort. There is nothing more for you to desire. How, indeed, can care come in through these golden doors, and sit upon your brow, and weigh you down with heaviness?"

"I will tell you," answered the king, "for I know that I can trust your good judgment. Here in my palace are all the noblest princes of Hellas suing for the hand of Helen, whom the gods have cursed with more than mortal beauty. Each has offered me a price, and each expects to win her. I dare not withhold her long; for then all will become angered, and my kingdom as well as my daughter will be the prey of him who is the strongest. I dare not give her to one of them, for then the other nine and twenty will make cause against me and bring ruin to Lacedæmon. On this side grin the heads of Scylla, all black with death; on that side dread Charybdis roars; and there is no middle way. Why, oh, why did not the immortals bless my daughter by giving her a homely face?"

Then Odysseus drew nearer to the king, and spoke in lower tones. "I pray you, do not despair," he said. "There is a safe way out of all this trouble. If you will only trust me, I will lead the whole matter to a happy issue."

"How, how?" eagerly asked the king.

"I will tell you," said Odysseus. "But you must first listen to a plea that I have to make. To you alone it is known that I am not a suitor for the hand of Helen, but that my hopes are all for coy Penelope. Speak to her father, your brother Icarius, and help me win her for my own, and I will settle this matter between you and the princely lovers of fair Helen in a manner pleasing to every one."

"It shall be as you wish!" cried the king, taking heart. "I will trust the management of this business to you, and may the wise Pallas Athené prosper you!"

The next morning shrewd Odysseus arose, and clothed himself in princely fashion; and, after the morning meal had been eaten, he bade the heralds call the suitors into the council chamber. And the heralds called the gathering; and the young heroes quickly came, one after another, until nine and twenty sat within the chamber where the elders of Lacedæmon were wont to meet. Then Odysseus stood on the raised platform, close to the door; and Pallas Athené, unseen by the dull eyes of mortals, stood beside him, and whispered words of wisdom in his ear.

"Noble men of Hellas," said Odysseus, "I pray that you will hearken to the words which I shall speak, and that you will duly weigh them in your minds. We have all come to Lacedæmon with one wish and one intent,—and that is, to win the most beautiful woman in the world. We have offered, each one for himself, a bride-price worthy of the bride; yet the king, for reasons which you ought to understand, is slow in bestowing her upon any of us. And so weeks and even months have passed, and we are still here, devouring the substance of our kind host, and yet as far as ever from the prize which we desire. Now, it behooves us to bring this matter to an end; for otherwise we all shall suffer loss by being too long absent from our homes."

The princely suitors listened kindly to his words and all nodded their assent. Then he went on:—

"Upon how many of you, now, has the peerless Helen smiled as if in admiration?"

Every man among them raised his hand in answer.

"Who, among you all, believes that fair Helen would prefer him, above every other, for a husband?"

Every man arose, and, glancing proudly around him, answered "I!"

"I have, then, a plan to offer," said Odysseus. "Let us leave the choice to Helen. And, in order that each may the better show whether there be aught of nobility in him, let us go forth straightway, and make trial of all the games in which any one of us excels. And when the games are ended, let glorious Helen come and choose him whom she will wed."

At this all the suitors shouted assent; for each felt sure that he would be the chosen one.

"But hearken to one word more!" cried Odysseus. "The most beautiful woman in the world is a prize of priceless value; and he who wins that prize will hardly keep it through the might of his unaided arm. Let us bind ourselves by an oath that he whom Helen chooses shall be her wedded husband, and that the rest will depart at once from Lacedæmon; and that if any man, from near or far, shall carry peerless Helen from her husband or her husband's home, then we will join our forces, and never falter in the fight until we have restored her to him."

"And further still," added Ajax Telamon, "let us swear that should any one of us forget the agreement made this day, then the remaining nine and twenty will cause swift punishment, and terrible, to fall upon him."

Much more did shrewd Odysseus and the assembled princes say; and in the end they made a solemn sacrifice to Father Zeus, and lifting up their hands they swore that they would hold to all that had been spoken. Then, at an hour which had been set, they went out to make trial of their skill in all kinds of manly games, so that each might show wherein he excelled all other men, and thus stand higher in the regards of matchless Helen. And the heralds made announcement, and a great company followed them to the broad marketplace between the palace and the city walls. King Tyndareus, happy that his perplexities were soon to end, sat upon a high throne overlooking the place; and at his side stood the glorious twins, Castor and Polydeuces, clad in their snow-white armor. But Helen, dowered with beauty by the gods, stood with her maidens at the window of her high-built chamber, and watched the contest from afar.

Then all the suitors, arrayed in princely garments, as became the mightiest men of Hellas, stood up in the lists, each for himself to take his part in the games. And each fondly believed that he, among them all, was the favored suitor of fair Helen. But shrewd Odysseus kept his own counsels, and wisely planned to reach the ends which he so much desired.

Then the games began. And they made trial, first, in throwing the heavy spear; and gray-bearded Idomeneus led all the rest. Then in shooting with the bow; and Odysseus was far the best, for no one else could string or handle the matchless bow of Eurytus. Then in throwing heavy weights; and Ajax, son of Telamon, sent a huge stone hurtling from his strong arms far beyond all other marks. Then in wrestling; and there was not one that could withstand the stout-limbed son of Oileus. Then in boxing; and Philoctetes, the armor-bearer of Heracles, carried off the palm. Then in fencing with the broad-sword; and Diomede held the championship, and found no peer. Then in leaping; and Thoas of Ætolia, one of the later comers, excelled all others. Then in the foot-race; and here again the lesser Ajax left all the rest behind.

And now the car of Helios was sloping towards the western sea, and King Tyndareus by a signal ordered that the games should cease.

"Come, my friends," said he, "the day is spent, and nothing can be gained by further trials of strength and skill. Let us go forthwith to my banquet hall, where the tables groan already with the weight of the good cheer which has been provided for you. And when you have rested yourselves, and put away from you the thought of hunger, fair Helen will descend from her high chamber, and choose from among you him who shall be her husband."

And all obeyed, and went straightway to the great banquet hall of the king. Now the court, and the hall, and even the passage-ways of the palace, were thronged with people old and young, noble and base-born; for all had heard of what was to follow. And the steward of the king had slain a score of long-wooled sheep, and many swine, and two slow-footed oxen; and these he had flayed and dressed for the goodly banquet. Then all sat down at the tables, and stretching forth their hands, they partook of the pleasant food so bounteously spread before them. And though some of the princely suitors had been beaten in the games, yet all were merry and hopeful, and many a pleasant jest was bandied back and forth among them.

"The son of Oileus should remember," said Nireus, "that the race is not always to the swift."

"And Nireus should remember," said Thoas, "that beauty does not consort with comeliness. Aphrodite did not choose Apollo for her husband, but rather the limping smith, Hephaestus."

Then some one asked Nireus what was the price of hair-oils in Syma; and this led to much merriment and many jokes about his smooth curls, his well-shaven face, and his tight-fitting doublet.

"If his father were living," said one, "he would be setting a bride-price upon him."

In the midst of the merriment, a herald passed through the hall, crying out, "Remember your oaths, O princes of the Hellenes! Remember your promises to the immortal gods!"

A silence fell upon that multitude, like the stillness which takes hold upon all nature when waiting for the thunder-cloud to vent its fury upon the plains. And the minstrel, who sat upon a raised seat at the farther side of the hall, touched his harp with his deft fingers, and brought forth sounds so sweet and low and musical that the ears of all the hearers were entranced. Then the door of the inner chamber opened, and the glorious Helen, leaning on the arm of old Tyndareus, came forth to make her choice. The hearts of all the suitors stood still; they could not bear to look toward her, although her heavenly beauty was modestly hidden beneath her thick veil. She came into the hall: she passed Idomeneus, who sat nearest the inner chamber; she passed the mighty Ajax, him of the noble form and the eagle eye; she passed the doughty Diomede, wielder of the sword; she passed Philoctetes, and Odysseus, and the stout-limbed son of Oileus. The hearts of the younger suitors on the hither side of the hall began to heat with high hopes.

"She surely has her eyes on me!" said the coxcomb Nireus, speaking to himself.

She came to the table where Menelaus, the brother of Agamemnon, sat. She paused a moment, and then she held out her lily-white hand, in token that he was the husband of her choice. The great silence was at once broken, and a mighty shout went up to the high roof of the palace. Every one of the slighted suitors felt for an instant the keen pang of disappointment; then, remembering their oaths, all joined in wishing joy to Menelaus and his bride. Some, however, chagrined and crestfallen, soon withdrew from the palace; and calling their servitors about them, they secretly and in haste departed from Lacedæmon. When the morning dawned, only ten of the young princes still staid in the halls of old Tyndareus.

It was easy to understand why these remained. Sweet-faced Penelope had won other hearts beside that of young Odysseus. "Since the glorious Helen is to be the bride of Menelaus," said each of those who tarried, "why shall not her fair cousin—who is worthier if not so beautiful—be mine to wed?"

And straightway they beset Icarius with offers of rich gifts, begging him to set a bride-price on his daughter, and bestow her upon him who should agree most willingly to pay it. The old man was sorely troubled, for he loved his daughter dearly; and he could not bear the thought that a strange prince should lead her into distant lands where, perchance, his eyes should never more behold her.

While he pondered sadly, sitting alone and bewildered in his chamber, he heard a minstrel singing in the hall. He listened. It was a song about Atalanta the fair huntress of Arcadia, beginning with the time when Meleager of the golden hair awarded her the prize in the far-off wood of Calydon.

Then the minstrel sang of the maiden's return to Arcadia: How she had stopped at Delphi on her way, and had asked the Pythia in Apollo's temple to reveal the secrets of her future life. How the oracle could tell her nothing of the things that would befall her, but only gave her this advice: "Keep thyself from wedlock's chains!" How, when she came again to her father's palace, she found him beset by suitors asking for the hand of his fleet-footed daughter. Then the maiden, calling to mind the Pythia's warning, besought her father to send the suitors home, and let her, like Artemis, live unwedded; for she would be as free as the winds which play in the lovely vales of Mantinea, or beat the bleak tops of Mount Enispe. But old Iasus was a crafty man—an unfeeling father, loving gold more than his daughter. "Behold," said he, "the bride-price that is offered. Shall I refuse so great gain, simply to please thy silly whims?" Then Atalanta was sorely troubled, and she prayed Artemis, the huntress-queen, to send her help in the time of her great need. And Artemis hearkened, and spoke words of comfort to her heart; and kind Pallas Athené gave her wisdom.

"My father," said she to old Iasus, "take thou the bride-price that any suitor may offer for me— but on these conditions: that he shall make trial with me in the foot-race, and if he outrun me, then I will go with him as his bride; but if I outstrip him in the race, then he is to lose the bride-price offered, and his life is to be at your mercy."

Crafty Iasus was highly pleased, and he rubbed his palms together with delight; and he caused the heralds to proclaim the terms on which the matchless Atalanta might be won. Some of the suitors departed in despair, for they knew that no mortal man was so fleet of foot as the lovely huntress of Arcadia. But many others, less wise, put themselves in training for the trial. Then one by one, like silly moths plunging into the candle's flame, they went down to the race-course of old Iasus, and tried their speed with that of the wing-footed damsel; but all failed miserably, and none of them ever returned to their homes or their loving friends. And Iasus grew rich upon the spoils—the jewels, and the bride-gifts, and the arms—which he thus gained from the luckless lovers.

One day Milanion, a youth from distant Scandia, came to try his fortune. "Knowest thou the terms?" asked Iasus.

"I know them," was the answer, "and though they were thrice as hard, yet would I win Atalanta."

And Atalanta, when she saw his manly, handsome face, and heard his pleasant voice, was sad to think that one so noble and so brave should meet so hard a fate. But Milanion went down to the race-course with a firm step and a heart full of hope. For he had prayed to Aphrodite that she would kindly aid his suit, and lend him wings to reach the goal in advance of Atalanta; and Aphrodite had listened to his plea, and had given him three golden apples, and had whispered a secret in his ear.

The signal was given, and youth and maiden bounded from the lists like arrows shot from a bow. But the maiden was much the fleeter of the two, and was soon far in advance.

"Another fool will soon come to grief!" said Iasus, laughing loudly.

By this time Atalanta was near the turning-post, while Milanion, straining every nerve, was many yards behind. Then he remembered the secret which Aphrodite had whispered, and he threw one of the golden apples far beyond the post. It fell upon the green lawn, a stone's-throw outside of the course. The quick eyes of Atalanta marked its beauty, and she ran to pick it up. And while she was seeking it among the grass, Milanion passed the turning-post, and was speeding swiftly back towards the goal. It was only a moment, however, until Atalanta swift as the wind overtook him, and was again far in the lead. Then the young man threw a second apple, this time some distance to the right of the course. The maiden followed, catching it almost before it fell; but Milanion had gained a hundred paces on her. Ere she could again overtake him, he threw his third apple over his shoulder and to the left of the course. Atalanta, forgetting in her eagerness that the goal was so near, stopped to secure this prize also; and lo! as she lifted her eyes, Milanion had reached the end of the course. Old Iasus stormed with rage, and threatened many fearful things. But Milanion, smiling, came boldly forward and claimed his bride; and she, blushing and happy, covered her face with her veil, and followed him willingly to the home of his fathers, in distant Cythera.

Such was the song which the minstrel sang, and to which Icarius listened while sitting in his chamber. Suddenly a new thought seemed to strike him, and he bade a herald call before him all the suitors of sweet Penelope.

"My young friends," he said, "you have asked me for my daughter's hand, and promised me a liberal bride-price. I need none of your gold, nor do I wish to give my daughter to a stranger with whom she would be loath to go. Hence I shall do after this manner: He who shall win in a foot-race to-day, on the long course beyond the market-place, shall be husband of Penelope, but on this condition: that, if she choose to go with him, then he is to have her without the payment of a price; but if she choose to stay with me, then he shall pay me a rich dower, and straightway depart forever from the gates of Lacedæmon."

The suitors heard the words of old Icarius, and all assented. Then soon the people were gathered again in the broad market-place; the long racecourse was cleared and put in order, and every thing was made ready for the trial. The trumpet sounded, and the young princes came forward lightly clad for the race. Palamedes, the cousin of Menelaus, fair and tall; and Ajax Oileus, who had won the race on the preceding day; and Megas, brave as Mars, from far Dulichium; and Thoas, the Ætolian prince; and

Phidippus, the grandson of great Heracles; and Protesilaus, from distant Thessaly; and Eumelus, son of Admetus and the divine Alcestis; and Polypoetes, descended from the Lapith king Peirithous and Hippodameia the daughter of the Centaurs; and Elphenor, the son of large-souled Chalcodon, ruler of Eubœa and the valorous Abantes; and lastly, Odysseus, who had shrewdly planned all matters to this end. Rarely have ten men so noble stood up together to contend for honors or the winner's prize.

The word was given, and they darted forth, at once and swiftly, raising a cloud of dust along the course. From the very start, they strained at utmost speed; they reached the turning-post, and hurried onward to the goal. But now stout Ajax no longer took the lead; for Odysseus ran before the rest, and passed the goal, and came to the crowd by the lists, while yet the others with laboring breath were speeding down the course.

Old Icarius was pleased with the issue of the race. For he hoped that Penelope would not consent to wed Odysseus and follow him to distant Ithaca; and, if so, he would be happily rid of all the troublesome suitors.

"Come here, my sweet daughter," he said. "This young man, a stranger from a far-off land, has won thee in the games; yet the choice is thine. Wilt thou leave thy old father, lonely and alone in Lacedæmon, preferring to share the fortunes of this stranger? Or wilt thou stay with me, and bid him seek a wife among the daughters of his own people?"

And sweet Penelope covered her face with her veil to hide her blushes, and said, "He is my husband; I will go with him."

Icarius said no more. But on that spot he afterwards raised a marble statue—a statue of Penelope veiling her blushes—and he dedicated it to Modesty.

Soon afterward Odysseus returned with his young wife to his own home and friends in sea-girt Ithaca. And, next to Penelope, the richest treasure that he carried thither was the bow of Eurytus.

ADVENTURE XIV

HOW A GREAT HERO MET HIS MASTER

NOW, after two years and more had passed in peace, there came one day to Ithaca an aged wanderer who had many things of great import to tell. For he had been in every land and in every clime, and had trod the streets of every city, even from Pylos to Iolcos by the sea; and he knew what deeds had been done by all the heroes, and what fortunes or misfortunes had befallen mankind in every part of Hellas. And Odysseus and the elders of Ithaca loved to sit around him in the banquet chamber of Laertes, and listen to his stories, of which there was no end. For in that wonderful Golden Age, these strollers—blind bards and storytellers—were the people's newspapers, and oftentimes the only means by which those of one country could learn aught of what was passing in another.

"Alas! the world is no longer as it was in the days of my youth," said the old newsmonger, one morning, with a sigh. "The heroes are all passing away. Indeed, of the older race, I can now remember only three who are still living,—Peleus, the king of the Myrmidons; Nestor, of lordly Pylos; and Laertes, in whose halls we are sitting."

"You forget Cheiron, the wise master," said Odysseus.

"By no means," was the answer. "It is now seven years since Zeus took him from earth, and set him among the stars. Some say that Heracles, while fighting with unfriendly Centaurs, unwittingly struck the great master with one of his poisoned arrows. Others say that the master, while looking at an arrow, carelessly dropped it upon his own foot, thus wounding himself unto death. But who is right, I cannot tell. I only know that Cheiron lives no longer in his cave-hall on rugged Pelion, and that the old heroes are all fast following him to the land of the unknown."

"But what of Neleus, the old father of Nestor? And what of my dear friend Iphitus of Œchalia? And what of great Heracles? Surely the race of heroes still lives in them."

"Can it be that you have not heard the sad story?" asked the old man. "Can it be that no one has yet brought to you the strange news, over which all Hellas has been weeping? Two harvests now have passed since the noble spirit of Iphitus fled down the dark ways,— it may be to the gloomy halls of Hades, it may be to the dwelling-place of fair-haired

Rhadamanthus in the Islands of the Blest. And old Neleus followed swiftly in his footsteps, his feeble life snuffed out by the mad hand of Heracles. Nor did great Heracles himself long survive the evil deed and the wrath of the eternal powers. But now he sits enthroned on high Olympus, and walks the earth no more."

"Pray tell us how it all came about," said King Laertes anxiously.

Then the old news-monger, prefacing his story with a sad, wild song, told how the greatest hero of the Golden Age met at last his master, even Death, the master of all earth's creatures. And this was the story that he told:—

"When Heracles fled from Calydon, as you already know, he went to Trachis in Thessaly, close by the springs of Œta; and there he abode a long time. Yet his mind was ill at rest, and dire forebodings filled his soul; for cruel Here was threatening him with madness, such as had once before darkened his life, and driven him to deeds too terrible to think upon. And so, at length, he kissed his dear wife and his lovely babies, and went forth to wander once more in loneliness from land to land. He knew that he would not return; and, unknown to Deianeira, he left in his dwelling a letter, such as men write when they feel that the end is drawing nigh. In it he told how the doves in the old oaks of Dodona had shown him that within the space of a year and three months he should depart from this earth; and then he gave directions how his goods should be given to his children and his friends, and what they should do to hold his memory in honor.

"After this he took ship, and came by sea to his old home at Tiryns, where erstwhile he had served his brother and task-master, Eurystheus. There he sojourned many days; and there he met Iphitus of Œchalia, his friend in early youth, seeking twelve horses of great worth and beauty, which had been stolen from him.

" 'Go you to Pherae in Messene,' said Heracles, his mind even then verging towards madness. 'It may be that the beasts have been taken by the lawless men of that country, for they live by robbery. But if you fail to find your horses there, come again to Tiryns, and report to me; and then I will aid you, even though we should have to seek them in the pasture-lands of old Autolycus beneath the shallow of Parnassus.'

"So Iphitus, with a score of his bravest followers, went down into Messene and Laconia, and even to the gates of Lacedæmon, looking for his horses. But he found no traces of the beasts; and in time he came again to Tiryns, as the great hero had directed him.

"Sad, however, was the day of his return, for the mind of Heracles was shrouded in deep darkness. While Iphitus sat as a guest at his table, the mighty son of Zeus arose in his madness, and slew him; and Heracles cared not for the vengeance of the gods, nor for the honor of his own board. Moreover, the goodly horses of Iphitus were even then feeding in his stables at Tiryns, for Heracles himself had found them.

"But after this the light began to struggle feebly in his mind, and the thought of his crime bore heavily upon him. Then he remembered old Neleus, the most ancient of men, and knew that he sat in the market-place at Pylos dealing out justice to all who came to him. And straightway he went by the nearest road to Pylos, and besought Neleus the venerable to purify him for the evil deed that he had done. But Iphitus and his father, old Eurytus, had been very dear to Neleus,—comrades and friends, indeed, in the stirring days of their youth.

" 'The blood of good Iphitus be upon you,' said the old man to Heracles; and he would not purify him, neither would he comfort him with words of kindness.

"Then madness again overpowered the great hero, and in his wrath he marched through Pylos breathing slaughter. And he slew old Neleus in the market-place, and put his sons and the elders of Pylos to the sword, sparing only the knightly Nestor, most discreet of men. But the fury of the great hero was not to run unchecked. The ever-living powers can never look with favor upon that man who slays his guest in his halls or who deals harshly with old age. And so they caused Heracles to be sold to Omphalé, queen of Lydia, to serve her as a bond-slave for a year and a day. And in that far-distant land he toiled at many a thankless task until the days of his bondage were ended. Yet the great cloud was only a little way lifted from his mind, and he thought to himself that all the misery that had ever been his had come upon him through the house of Eurytus. So he swore with a great oath, that, when he had gotten his freedom, he would utterly destroy Œchalia, and would sell all its people into bondage. For, in a dazed, unreasoning way, he remembered fair Iole, and the slight which Eurytus had put upon him when he made trial of his skill in archery.

"Now, when he was set free, he remembered all too well the vow which he had made; and when he had overthrown Œchalia, and had taken captive all the fair women and children, he bethought him that he would go again to Trachis where his wife and children still dwelt. But on his way thither he stopped for a time in Eubœa to offer sacrifice to Zeus; and he sent his herald Lichas on before him, with certain of the captives. When Lichas came to Trachis, and made himself known to Deianeira, she asked him what word he had brought from Heracles his master.

" 'He is alive and well,' said the herald, 'and he tarries for a while in Eubœa to build an altar to Zeus.'

" 'Why does he do that?' asked Deianeira.

" 'He does it to fulfil a vow,' answered the herald,— 'a vow which he made ere yet he had overthrown Œchalia and had led captive these fair women whom thou seest.'

"Then Deianeira drew nearer, and looked with pity upon the captives as they stood in sad array on the shore of the desolate sea. And she lifted her hands toward heaven, and prayed that the great powers would keep her from such a fate and would shield her children that so sad an evil should never overtake them. Then she saw that one among the captives was much more beautiful than the others, tall and very fair, with long golden tresses, and eyes as round as the moon and as blue as the deep sea. And Deianeira, wondering whether she were not some great man's daughter, asked her who she was; but the sad captive answered not a word. The tender heart of the queen was filled with pity; and she bade that the beautiful lady should be taken into the great hall of Heracles, and treated with the utmost kindness, that so she should not have sorrow heaped upon sorrow. Then she asked Lichas to tell her who the lady was; but he said that he knew not, save that she seemed to be well born.

"But now when Lichas had gone to the tents by the shore, there came to Deianeira in the palace a mischief-maker who told her that Lichas had not answered truly in this matter.

" 'He knows, as well as I, who this fair stranger is,' said the mischief-maker. 'She is the daughter of King Eurytus of Œchalia, and the sister of Iphitus. Her name is Iole; and it was for the sake of her beauty that Heracles destroyed her father's city.'

"Then Deianeira was sadly troubled lest the heart of the great hero should be turned away from her, and his affections set upon this lovely captive. So she sent again for Lichas, and questioned him still further. At first he denied that he knew any thing about the fair lady; but afterwards, when hard pressed, he said, 'She is indeed Iole, the fair damsel whom Heracles loved in the springtime of youth. But why he has brought this great grief upon her, and upon her father's house, I cannot tell.'

"Sorely troubled now was Deianeira, and all day long she sat in her chamber, and pondered what she should do. And when the evening was come, she called her friends together, the women and maidens who dwelt in Trachis, and talked with them.

" 'I have been thinking of what I can do to keep my husband's love,' she said. 'I had almost forgotten that I have a charm which will help me, or I might not have been so sadly troubled. Years and years ago, when we were fleeing from my dear old home at Calydon, we came to the river Evenus. The water was very deep, and the current very swift; but there lived on the banks of the stream an old Centaur, named Nessus, whose business it was to ferry travellers across to the other shore. He first took my husband safely over, and then myself and our little son Hyllus. But he was so rude, and withal so savage in his manners, that Heracles was greatly angered at him; and he drew his bow, and shot the brutish fellow with one of his poisoned arrows. Then my woman's heart was filled with pity for the dying Centaur, wicked though he was; and I felt loath to leave him suffering alone upon the banks of Evenus. And he, seeing me look back, beckoned me to him. "Woman," he said, "I am dying; but first I would give thee a precious gift. Fill a vial with the blood that flows from this wound, and it shall come to pass that if ever thy husband's affections grow cold, it will serve as a charm to make him love thee as before. It needs only that thou shouldst smear the blood upon a garment, and then cause him to wear the garment so that the heat of the sun or of a fire shall strike upon it." I quickly filled the vial, as he directed, and hastened to follow my husband.'

"Then Deianeira called the herald Lichas, and said, 'Behold, here is a fair white garment which I have woven with my own hands; and I vowed many days ago, that, if my husband should again come home, I would give him this garment to wear while offering sacrifice. Now he tarries, as you say, to do homage to the gods in Eubœa. Go back, therefore, to meet him, and give him this white robe as a gift from his wife. Say to him that on no account shall he let another wear it; and that he shall keep it carefully folded up, away from the light and the heat, until he shall be ready to clothe himself in it.'

"The herald promised to do as he was bidden; and in that same hour he hastened back to meet his master in Eubœa, taking with him his master's young son Hyllus.

"Not many days after this, a great cry and sad bewailings were heard in the house of Heracles; and Deianeira rushed forth from her chamber crying aloud that she had done some terrible deed. 'For I anointed the fair robe which I sent to my husband with the blood of Nessus the Centaur; and now, behold, the bit of woollen cloth which I dipped into the charm, and used as a brush in spreading it upon the robe, is turned to dust, as if a fire had burned it up. I have not forgotten any thing that the Centaur told me: how I was to keep the charm where neither the light of the sun nor the heat of the fire could touch it. And this I have done until now; only the bit of woollen cloth was left lying in the sunshine. Oh, fearful am I that I have slain my husband! For why should the Centaur wish to do well by the man who brought death upon him?'

"Hardly had she spoken these words when her son Hyllus came in great haste to the palace, even into the woman's hall where she stood.

" 'O my mother!' he cried. 'Would that you were not my mother! For do you know that you have this day brought death and destruction upon my father.'

" 'Oh, say not so, my son,' wailed Deianeira. 'It cannot be!'

" 'But truly it is so,' said Hyllus. 'For when Lichas and myself came to Eubœa bearing the white robe which you sent, we found my father ready to begin his offering of sacrifices. And he was glad to see me and to hear from you; and he took the beautiful robe and put it upon him. Then he slew twelve fair oxen, and joyfully worshipped the ever-living powers. But when the fire grew hot, the deadly robe began to cling to him, and pangs, as if caused by the stings of serpents, shot through him, and the pains of death seized on him. He asked Lichas why he had brought that robe; and when the herald told him that it was your gift, he seized the wretch, and cast him over the cliff upon the sharp rocks beneath. And great fear filled the hearts of all who saw the sufferings of the mighty hero; and none of them dared come near him, so terrible were his struggles. Then he called to me, and said, "Come here, my son. Do not flee from your father in his great distress; but carry me from this land, and set me where the eyes of no man shall see me." And so we put him in the hold of our good ship, and brought him home with us to Trachis. And soon you shall see what you have done; for you have slain your husband,—a hero the like of whom the world shall never see again.'

"When Deianeira heard these words she made no answer, but, with one despairing cry, she hasted to her high-built chamber; and when, soon afterward, her maidens sought her there, she was dead. Then Hyllus came, also seeking her; for the women of the household had told him how she had been deceived by the dying Centaur. And when he saw her lifeless form, he wept bitterly, and cried out that now indeed the Fates had bereft him of both father and mother on the same day.

"Then they brought Heracles into his own broad hall, bearing him upon a litter. He was asleep; for the pain had left him a little while, and tired Nature was taking her dues. But the sad wailings of his son awoke him; and again he cried aloud in his agony, and besought those who stood around him that they would give him a sword wherewith to end his pain. Then Hyllus came into the hall, and told his father all about the terrible mistake which his mother had made, and how the Centaur had deceived her, and how she was at that moment lying dead, with a broken heart, in the chamber overhead.

" 'Then, indeed, is my doom come,' cried Heracles. 'For long ago the oracles spake of me, that I should die, not by the hands of any living being, but by the guile of one dwelling in the regions of the dead. So now Nessus, whom I slew so long ago, is avenged; for he has slain me. Now, my son, carry me to the wooded summit of the hill of Œta, and build there a great pile of olive beams and of oak; and, when it is finished, lay me upon it, and set fire unto it. And shed no tear, neither utter any cry, but work in silence; for thus thou shalt prove thyself a son of Heracles.'

"The boy promised to do all this as his father wished, only he would not set fire to the pile. So when he had built the pile, and had put between the beams great stores of spices and sweet-smelling herbs, they laid Heracles upon it; and Philoctetes, the hero's armor-bearer, set fire to the pile. And Heracles, for this kindness, gave to Philoctetes his famous bow,—a weapon more marvellous even than the bow of Eurytus. Then the red flames shot high towards heaven, shedding brightness over land and sea; and the mighty hero was at rest. He had met his master."

Such was the story that the old news-monger told in the hall of King Laertes.

LONG LIVE THE KING!

"Surely," sighed Laertes, "the old heroes pass away; but the younger heroes press hard in their footsteps, and will fill their places well. The gods have written it in every tree, and upon every blade of grass, that the aged, however worthy, cannot endure forever. The ripened fruit falls to the ground, but there will be other and better fruit on the branches by and by. Ancient Cronos gave place, not willingly, to Zeus; and Zeus is by far the greater of the two. And there be certain oracles which have foretold the doom of Zeus; even that he shall be hurled from his throne by a king of peace, who shall reign ever-lastingly."

Then on a day, he called the elders of Ithaca together, and spoke to them in this wise: "My son Odysseus is now a grown-up man, wise and shrewd beyond any other among you. He is skilled in all kinds of knowledge and of handicraft; in matters of judgment he is without a peer, and in matters requiring courage he is foremost among men. More-over, he is married to a wife, sweet Penelope,

183

unexcelled in wifely virtues; and he has a son and heir, Telemachus,—a smiling babe who has not yet seen the round of one full moon. Now, why should the old branch stand longer in the way of the new and vigorous shoot? This day I will give up my king-dom to my son, and he shall henceforth rule this island in his own name."

And all the people rejoiced when they heard his words; and straightway they hailed Odysseus king of Ithaca, and offered thanksgiving and sacrifice to Pallas Athené, who had blessed him with wisdom above that of other men. And good Laertes retired to his mountain farm, where no vexing questions of government would take him away from his vines and fruit-trees. "Here," said he, "I hope to end my days in peace."

When the men of Cephallenia and the dwell-ers in the rugged island of Zacynthus heard that young Odysseus ruled by his own right in Ithaca, they came and offered him their friendship and allegiance; for they were kinsmen of the Ithacans. They brought rich presents of corn and wine and of long-wooled sheep, and promised to bear him aid in time of need, if ever that time should come.

At about this time, old Icarius, the father of Penelope, came to Ithaca for a brief visit to his daughter. For his eyes had long yearned to see her, and he could find no rest until he knew that she was happy and well cared for in the new home which she had chosen. And Penelope asked him a thousand questions about her friends and her kinsfolk in dear old Lacedæmon, and to all these questions he made answer as he best knew.

"We have now a new king at Lacedæmon," said Icarius, "even brave Menelaus, the husband of your cousin Helen."

"But where is King Tyndareus, my good uncle?" asked Penelope. "And where are my noble twin cousins, Castor and Polydeuces? Do they share the kingdom with Menelaus?"

"I will tell you all about it," answered her father. And then he told her how it had come about that Menelaus was called to the kingship of Lacedæmon:—

"As the feebleness of age began to take hold upon him, King Tyndareus bethought him that he would resign his kingdom to his sons, the twin heroes Castor and Polydeuces. But the restless youths cared not to take upon them duties which would keep them within the narrow bounds of Lacedæmon; for they were not home-stayers, but they wandered hither and thither over many seas and through strange lands, doing brave and noble deeds innumerable. The story of their labors in times of peace and of their prowess in times of war was upon every tongue, and was sung by minstrels in every city of Hellas. Wherever public games were held, there the twins were the masters of the course and the field, and the awarders of the prizes. Wherever battles raged and where the fight was thickest, there the glorious heroes, on their snow-white steeds, were seen striking fearlessly for the cause of right. And men told how it was they who first taught the bards to sing songs of battle and pæans of victory; and how it was they who first showed the glad feet of the victors how to tread the wild mazes of the war-dance; and how it was they who, in their friendship for seafarers, had guided many a vessel over the roughest seas, safe into the wished-for haven. They belonged not more to their native Lacedæmon than to the whole wide world.

"There came a time, however, when the men of Laconia quarrelled with their neighbors of Arcadia, and there was war upon the borders. Then Castor and Polydeuces hastened to take sides with their kinsmen. Mounted on their swift steeds, Phlogios and Harpagos, the gifts of Hermes, they made raid after raid across the mountains; and they brought back many a choice herd of cattle, or flock of sheep, from the pasture-lands of Arcadia.

"It happened on a day, that their cousins Idas and Lynceus, two lawless men from Messene, joined them, and the four drove many cattle across the borders, and hid them in a glen at the foot of Mount Taygetus. Then they agreed that Idas should divide the booty into four parts, and give to each a part. But Idas was a crafty man, more famed for his guile than for his courage; and he planned how he might take all the herd for his own. So he killed a fat ox, and having flayed and dressed it, he cut it into four parts. Then he called the other men about him.

" 'It would be a great pity to divide so fine a herd as this of ours among four owners,' he said. 'Therefore I have a plan by which one, or at most two of us, may fairly gain the whole. Behold, here are the four quarters of the ox which I have slain. This quarter belongs to Castor, this to Polydeuces, this to Lynceus, and this to myself. He who first eats the share allotted to him shall have half of the cattle for his own; he who next finishes shall have the other half.'

"Then, without another word, he began to eat the quarter which he had allotted to himself; nor was he long devouring it, but with greedy haste consumed it before his comrades had tasted even a morsel. Next he seized upon the part assigned to Lynceus, and ate it as quickly as his own.

" 'The cattle are all mine!' he cried. And calling upon his brother to help him, they drove the whole herd into Messene.

"Then anger filled the souls of the twin heroes, and they vowed to take vengeance upon their crafty kinsmen. One night when the moon lighted up both plain and mountain with her silvery beams, they made a rapid ride into Messene, and brought back not only the herd which Idas had taken from them by fraud, but as many cattle as were feeding in the Messenian meadows. Then, knowing that their cousins would follow them in hot haste, they hid themselves in the hollow of a tree in the mountain pass, and waited for the morning.

"At break of day, the two Messenians, having missed their cattle, hastened to follow their trail to Mount Taygetus. Then Lynceus, whose sharp eyes could see through rocks and the trunks of trees, climbed to the top of a crag to look about them; for they feared lest they should fall into an ambush. And as he peered into every nook and glen and gorge of the wild mountain, he saw the twins close-hidden in the hollow trunk of an oak. Then quickly he descended, and with stealthy tread he and Idas drew near their hiding-place. Castor saw them first; but before he could speak, a spear from the hand of Idas laid him low in death. Then mighty Polydeuces leaped forth in his wrath, and rushed upon the slayers of his brother. Fear seized upon them, and they fled with winged feet into Messene, and paused not until they stood by the marble tomb of their father, great Aphareus. But Polydeuces, following on, overtook them there, and with his spear smote Lynceus a deadly blow. At the same time, a peal of thunder shook the mountain and rolled over the plain; and Zeus hurled his fiery bolts at the bosom of crafty Idas, and laid him dead upon his father's tomb.

"The grief of Polydeuces for the death of Castor was terrible to see; and there was no one in all the world who could comfort him, or in any way make him forget his loss. Then he prayed the gods that they would take him, too, to Hades, that he might be in the dear company of his brother. And Zeus heard his prayer; and he asked Polydeuces to choose whether he would sit in the courts of

Olympus, and be the peer of Ares and Pallas Athené, or whether he would share all things with Castor. And the glorious hero cried, 'Let me be forever with my brother!' His wish was granted to him; and the twin heroes still live, although the quickening earth lies over them. One day they wander in the fields of asphodel, and enjoy the bliss of immortality; the next, they flit among the unquiet shades in the sunless regions of the dead. And thus they share together whatever of joy or woe the grave can bring.

"When King Tyndareus learned that he was bereft of his sons, he fell prone to the earth; and no one in Lacedæmon could console him. 'Send for Helen, my peerless daughter!' he cried. 'Send for Menelaus. He is my only son. He shall dwell in my palace, and rule in my stead!'

"And that is the way in which it came about, that Menelaus was called to the kingship of Lacedæmon."

Old Icarius remained but a short time at Ithaca. A ship was waiting in the harbor, ready to sail to Pylos and the ports beyond; and he knew that a like opportunity to return to Lacedæmon might not soon be offered. And so, leaving his blessing with his children Odysseus and Penelope and the babe Telemachus, he departed.

ADVENTURE XVI

THE CHILDREN OF PROMETHEUS

THERE was sore distress in Lacedæmon. Famine and a deadly pestilence grieved the land, and in every household the notes of wailing and despair were heard. For Apollo, vexed because the men of Laconia were so slow to understand his wishes, was shooting his fateful arrows broadcast among them. Like a night-cloud he brooded over the land, and strong men and fair women and helpless babes all fell alike beneath the sharp blows of his deadly shafts. And the heart of Menelaus the king was burdened with grief because of the people's sore affliction. Then, when he found that sacrifice of lambs and goats availed him nothing, he sent in haste to ask the oracles the cause of Apollo's wrath, and to learn what could be done to stay the plague. The answer came as quickly:—

"When the bones of the children of Prometheus are brought from Ilios, and entombed in Lacedæmon, then the wrath of silver-bowed

Apollo shall be turned aside, and the smiles of his favor shall bless the land."

Then Menelaus made ready to depart at once to Troy to do that which Apollo demanded. A short journey by land brought him to the strong-built town of Helos on the shore of the eastern sea. There a swift-sailing ship lay at its moorings, while a score of long-haired seamen paced the beach, anxious to embark upon any errand across Poseidon's watery kingdom. The captain hailed the king with joy, and the ship was soon made ready for the long voyage to Ilios. A plenteous stock of food was stored away in the broad hold; arms, for defence against sea robbers and savage men, were put in order, and hung in their places; and rich presents for Priam, king of Troy, were taken on board.

The next day a favoring wind sprang up; the sails were set; the seamen took their places; and the ship with King Menelaus on board sped on its way to distant Ilios. Poseidon, looking out from his golden palace beneath the sea, saw the vessel as it hastened on its errand; and he bade the waves be still and in no wise hinder its speed, for Apollo's business must not be delayed; and he called upon the breezes to blow steadily towards Ilios, that so the embassy of Menelaus might be happily performed.

"Surely the gods are all in league with us," said the captain of the ship one day, pleased with the delightful voyage. "To-morrow we shall doubtless sight the Lesbian coast, and from thence it is but a short sail to Ilios and Troy. And now, as we sit together in the prow of our good vessel, I pray you to tell us the story, once more, of great Prometheus, the bones of whose children seem so precious to Apollo."

And Menelaus willingly consented, and told the story as he himself had oft-times heard it from the bards:—

"When Zeus waged pitiless war upon the Titans, and hurled them headlong from the heights of Mount Olympus, he spared from the general ruin those who fought not with their own kindred, but espoused his cause. Among these and foremost of all was great Prometheus, whose name is Forethought, and whose chiefest glory lies in this, that he was the friend and lover of man-kind. It was the hope of bettering man's condition that led him to fight against his kindred, and to aid in placing Zeus upon the throne of ancient Cronos. Yet Zeus cared naught for the feeble children of earth, but sought rather to make their burdens heavier and their lives more sad, that so the race might perish utterly. And the great mind of Prometheus set to work to learn how to make their lot less sad and their lives less miserable.

He saw that as yet they dwelt without forethought upon the earth, their life's whole length being aimless, and their minds as void of reason as is the beast's. They lived in sunless caverns, or in holes scooped in the ground; and no provision did they make for heat or cold or times of scarcity, or the varying needs of youth and age. And Prometheus wasted no vain words in pity, but took at once upon him the Titanic task of lifting the race up to a level with the gods. First, he taught them the use of fire, which, some say, he stole from Helios' car, and brought to the earth, hidden in a fennel-stalk. Then he showed them how the stars rise and set, and how the seasons change in never-varying order. He showed them how to yoke and make submissive to their will the wild steeds of the desert plain; how to turn the sod beneath the soil by means of the furrowing plough; and how to build fair houses, and cities with strong walls and frowning towers. He taught them how to make ships, the storm-winged chariots of the sea, and how to navigate the briny deep. He showed them the treasures which lie hidden underneath the ground,—gold, silver, iron,— and taught them how to turn them into forms of beauty, strength, and use. In short, all arts now known to men came to them from the hands and mind of pitying Prometheus.

"Now, when Zeus looked down from high Olympus, and saw the puny tribes of men no longer grovelling in the earth like senseless beasts, but standing upright, and claiming kinship with the gods, he shook with pent-up anger. And he called two of his mightiest servants, Strength and Force, whom none can resist, and bade them seize the friend of man, and bind him upon a peak of the snow-crowned Caucasus, there to linger through the ages in loneliness and pain.

"Then the ruthless slaves of Zeus went forth to do his bidding. They seized the mighty Titan, and dragged him to the bleak and barren regions of the Caucasus, beyond the utmost limit of the habitable earth. And with them went the mighty smith Hephaestus, all unwillingly, to bind the great victim with bonds of brass, which none could loose, to the lonely mountain-crags.

" 'This thing I do loathing,' said Hephaestus. 'Here I must perforce leave thee, chained and bolted to the immovable rocks. Thou shalt never behold the face of man, nor hear the accents of his voice; but the blaze of the unpitying sun shall scorch thy fair skin, and thou shalt long for the night with its shimmering stars to cast a veil of coolness over thee. Year after year, thou shalt keep thy lonely watch in this joyless place, unblest with sleep, and uttering many a cry and unavailing moan. For Zeus is pitiless. This is what thou gainest for befriending man.'

"There, then, they left him fettered; but not until rude Strength had taunted him: 'Lo, thou lover of mankind! Call now the puny race of mortals round thee, and crown them with honors! Could all of them together lessen thy punishment in the least? Surely the gods did jest when they gave thee the name of "Forethought," for thou hast need of forethought to free thee from these bonds.'

"Then, when the solitary sufferer knew that there was no one to hear him, save only the sun, and the earth and the winds, and the winding river and the distant sea, he broke forth in grievous cries and lamentations:—

" 'O pitying sky, and swift-winged winds, and river-springs, and the many-twinkling smile of ocean, I cry to you! O mother Earth, and thou all-seeing Sun! behold what I endure because I gave honor to mortals! Behold what torture is in store for me, while for ten thousand years I writhe in these unseemly chains! Yet the things that come are all foreknown to me, and nothing happens unexpected; and I must bear as best I may the ills that will perforce be mine, knowing that the end of all these things shall come to me at last.'

"Then the Ocean-nymphs, with the fragrance of flowers and a rustling sound like the whirr of birds, came floating through the air, and hovered about the crag where Prometheus was bound. They had heard the clank of the iron and the heavy blow of the sledge resounding to the very cavern-depths of Ocean; and they had hastened to come, and offer him their sympathy.

"Following them, came old Oceanus himself, riding in his winged chariot; for no firmer friend had Prometheus than this hoary-headed ancient of the encircling sea. He came to condole with the suffering Titan, and to counsel patience and submission. But he staid not long.

" 'I will drink the cup of bitterness to its very dregs,' said Prometheus, 'and will bide the time when Zeus shall have quenched his wrath.'

"And Oceanus, feeling that he had come in vain, turned about, and gladly hastened homeward to his halls beneath the ocean billows.

"After this many others came, weeping tears of sorrow for the sufferer,—tears of anger at the tyranny of Zeus. And wails of mourning were borne thither on the wings of the wind from all the tribes that dwelt in Asia,—from the warrior maidens on the Colchian coasts, from the savage horsemen of the Scythian plains, and from the dwellers on the farther shores of Araby. But the Titan, chained to the desolate crags, suffered on. Above him the vultures hovered, and the wild eagles shrieked; and sun and storm beat mercilessly upon his head, as the weary days and the lengthening years passed by. And yet no deliverance came.

"One day, as he writhed helplessly in his chains, Prometheus saw in the valley below him what at so great distance seemed to be a beautiful heifer, having a fair face like that of a woman. 'Surely,' said he aloud, 'it is the child of Inachus, she who warmed the heart of Zeus, and is now through Here's hate changed into an unseemly shape, and driven to weary wanderings.'

"Then the maiden gazed at him in wonder, and asked, 'Who are you whom the gods have doomed to suffer in this solitary place? And how came you to know my father's name, and the sorrows that have come upon me? And tell me, I pray, if such knowledge be yours, whether there shall ever be any help for me, and when my sufferings shall have an end.'

"The Titan answered, 'I who speak to thee am Prometheus, who brought down fire to men, and gave them knowledge, and taught them how to do godlike things. And I know that thou art Io, once the lovely daughter of Inachus, king of Argos; but what thou art now, let thy own lips speak and answer.'

" 'I cannot choose but tell you all,' the maiden answered, 'though my speech shall with sobs be broken when I recall the memory of happy days forever gone. There was a time when in my father's halls I dwelt in maidenly freedom, a spoiled and petted child. But as I grew to womanhood, dreams came to me which told me that I was beloved by Zeus. Such trouble did these visions bring to me, that I was fain to tell my father of them. He knew not what to do. But he sent swift messengers to Delphi and Dodona to ask the oracles what the dreams portended, and how he could best give pleasure to the gods. The answer came, that he should drive me from his doors into the wide and cruel world, or otherwise the fiery bolts of Zeus would burn up all his household and destroy him utterly. Reluctantly and weeping bitter tears, he shut me out; and lo! straightway my body was changed into the loathed form which stands before you, and a gad-fly stung me with its fangs, and I rushed away in madness, vainly hoping to find relief at Lerne's fountain water. But there the herdsman Argus, with his hundred eyes, did track me out; and with his scourge and the goading fly, I was driven along unending ways. Then Hermes, seeing my distress, took pity on me, and sought to free me from my cruel keeper. But Argus never slept; and with his hundred eyes he saw every danger, and shunned it while it was yet afar. At last Hermes bethought him of the power of music. Playing a soft melody on his lute, he stole gently towards the herdsman; the sweet sounds charmed the savage ear, and sleep overpowered the hundred eyes. Then Hermes drew his sword quickly, and smote off the head of Argus, thus gaining for himself the name of the Argusqueller. But the shade of the terrible herdsman still follows me, and I find no rest; and aimlessly I have come, thus goaded onward, to this wild mountain region.'

"Then Prometheus in pitying accents said, "Listen now to me, and I will tell thee, Io, what other sorrows thou must bear from Here; for it is she who brought this woe upon thee and who hounds thee thus from land to land. Thou shalt journey onward from these mountain regions through the Scythian land, and the region of the uncouth Chalybes who work in iron. Thence thou shalt cross the mountains to the dwelling-place of the Amazons, who shall lead thee to the place where the ocean-gates are narrowest. There thou shalt plunge into the waves, and swim with fearlessness of heart to Asia's shore. And that strait shall by its name, Bosphorus, tell to latest ages the story of thy wandering. But what I have told thee is only the beginning of thy doom.'

"Then Io wept.

" 'Were it not better to die,' she asked, 'than to endure this hopeless misery?'

" 'Not so, O maiden,' answered the Titan; 'for if thou livest then a son of thine shall loose me from my fetters, and perchance shall shake the throne of Zeus himself. When thou hast crossed the sea-ways which part the continent, thou shalt wander on until thou hast reached the outmost islands where the Gorgons dwell; then returning thou shalt pass through the country of the griffins and the region of Ethiopia, and shalt come at last to the three-cornered ground where flows the Nile. There thou shalt rest, and thy maiden form with all its comeliness shall be thine again. In Canobus, a fair city by the sea, shall a home be made for thee; and there shall Epaphos thy son be born, from whom in after-times shall spring great Heracles, who shall break my bonds and set me free from these hated fetters.'

"Then Io, with a sigh of mingled hope and despair, went on her weary way, and left Prometheus alone again in the everlasting solitudes. And the wild eagles swooped down from their high-built nests, and circled with threatening screams about him; a grim vulture flapped its wings in his face, and buried its talons in his bosom; a mighty storm came hurtling down through the mountain passes; the earth shook to and fro, and the peaks of Caucasus seemed as if toppling to their base; a hurricane of snow and hail and rattling ice smote the Titan about the head, and wrapped his body in eddying gusts; the lightnings leaped with lurid glare athwart the sky, and the thunders crashed with deafening roar among the crags; and earth and air and sea seemed blent together in a mighty turmoil, and whirling into utter chaos. Yet, in the midst of all, the old Titan quailed not; but with voice serene and strong he sang of the day when right shall triumph over might, when truth shall trample error in the dust, and the reign of Zeus give place to that of a nobler monarch just and perfect in all his ways.

"Thus years upon years passed, and ages circled by, until thirteen generations of men had lived and died upon the earth. Then came Heracles, the descendant of Io, to purge the world of vile monsters, and to give freedom to those who were in bonds. And as he wandered from land to land, to do the bidding of his master Eurystheus, he passed through Ethiopia, and came to the region of the Caucasus, close by the eastern Ocean's stream. There, as he gazed upward at the everlasting peaks, he saw the great Titan fettered to the naked rock, while the eagles circled about him, and the grim vulture digged its talons into his flesh; and Heracles knew that this was Prometheus the ancient, the friend of the human race and the foe of tyrants. He drew his bow, and with his unerring arrows slew the eagles and the vulture; and then, with mighty blows of his club, he broke the chains which Hephaestus of old had wrought, and with his strong hands he loosed the long-suffering prisoner from his fetters. And the earth rejoiced; and men everywhere sang pæans of triumph, because freedom had been given to him who raised them from the dust, and endowed them with the light of reason and the fire of god-like intelligence."

This was the tale which Menelaus told to a company of eager listeners seated about him, in the prow of the swift-sailing vessel.

"Now you should know," he added, "that every lover of freedom in Hellas is in truth a child of Prometheus. And so when Apollo, through his oracle, bade me fetch from Ilios the bones of the old Titan's children, I understood that I was to gather the dust of all the Hellenes who have died in the Trojan land, and carry it to Lacedæmon for honored burial. And such is the errand upon which we are sailing to-day."

"But why is it said that every Hellene is a child of Prometheus?" asked the captain. "Is it simply because he is a lover of freedom and a hater of tyrants, as the old Titan was? Or is there a real line of kinship reaching from us up to him?"

"I will tell you," answered the king. "While Prometheus hung fettered to the bleak crag of Caucasus, and in grim patience bided the day of deliverance, his son Deucalion tilled the plains of Phthia, and gathered the ripe fruits on its sunny hills. And he dwelt in peace with all men, cherishing in his heart the words which his father had spoken to him in former times. But the world was full of wicked-ness, and there was violence and bloodshed everywhere; and men no longer had respect for the gods, or love for one another. 'We are a law unto ourselves,' they cried. 'Why then should any one obey the behests of a master whom he has not seen?' And they went on eating and drinking and making merry, and gave no thanks to the giver of every good.

"At length, when their wickedness waxed so great that it was past all bearing, Zeus spoke the word, and a mighty flood burst upon the land. The west wind came sweeping in from the great sea, bringing in its arms dark clouds laden with rain. And when Deucalion saw the veil of darkness covering the sky, and heard the roar of the hurricane in the valley below him, he called to Pyrrha, his golden-haired wife, and said, 'Surely, now, the day has come of which my father told me often,—the day when floods of water shall come upon the earth to punish the wickedness of men. Hasten into the ark which I have built, that, if so be, we may save ourselves from the merciless waves.'

"And they made the ark ready, and put a great store of food in its broad hold, and waited for the rising of the waters. Nor was it long; for the torrents gushed down from the hillsides and filled the valleys, and the plains were covered over, and the forests sank from sight beneath the waves. But Deucalion and Pyrrha sat in the ark, and floated safely on the bosom of the heaving waters. Day after day they drifted hither and thither, until at last the ark rested on the lofty peak of Parnassus. Then Deucalion and

Pyrrha stepped out upon the dry ground; the rain ceased to fall, the clouds were scattered and the waters fled down the valleys and hastened to the sea; but all the people of Hellas, save only Deucalion and Pyrrha, had perished in the flood. And feeling their loneliness in the midst of the ruin and death which had come upon the land, these two built an altar to the gods, and offered thanks for their deliverance. Then Zeus sent Hermes, the bright messenger, to speak words of comfort to them.

" 'Among all the folk of this land,' he said, 'you alone have lived blameless lives, and with your clean hands and pure hearts have pleased the immortals. Ask now what you most desire, and it shall be given to you.'

"Then Deucalion wept as he bowed before the messenger. 'Grant that we may see the earth teeming again with busy men,' he said.

" 'It shall be as you wish,' answered Hermes. 'As you go down the mountain into the plain, cover your faces with your mantles, and throw the bones of your mother behind you.'

"Then the messenger left them, and they wondered between themselves what was the meaning of his words.

" 'Who is our mother?' asked Pyrrha.

" 'Is not the earth the mother of us all?' then answered Deucalion. 'His meaning is plain enough now.'

"So, as they went down Parnassus, they took up stones, and threw them behind them. And the stones which Deucalion threw sprang up and were mighty armed men; and those which Pyrrha threw became fair women. Thus the hills and the valleys were peopled anew; and the earth smiled, and was glad that a new and happier day had dawned.

"But Deucalion went with Pyrrha into Locris; and there he built the city of Opus, where he reigned king for many years; and there sons and daughters, noble and beautiful, were born; but the noblest was Hellen, from whom the Hellenes are descended, and our country of Hellas takes its name.

"Do you understand now how everyone of us can claim to be a son of great Prometheus?"

A CAUSE OF WAR

Time passed.

Menelaus had returned from Ilios, bringing with him the bones of his countrymen who had died in that distant land. The great plague had been stayed, for the anger of Apollo had been assuaged. And it had seemed for a time that the old days of peace and plenty had come again to Lacedæmon, never to depart.

Yet within a few weeks all was changed once more. There was silence in the golden halls of Menelaus, and guests sat no longer as of yore around the banquet tables. Anger and grief and uneasiness were plainly seen in every face. Men gathered in the streets, and talked in wild, excited tones about the strange things which had lately happened in Lacedæmon; and the words "Helen," and "Paris," and "Troy," and "Ilios" seemed to be on every tongue, and repeated with every sign of love and hatred, of admiration and anxiety.

"Our good king, by his visit to Troy, lifted the scourge of pestilence and famine from our land," said one of the elders of the city; "but he brought to our shores a greater evil,—even Paris, the handsome prince of Ilios. And now the glory of our country, the sun which delighted all hearts, the peerless Helen, has been stolen by the perfidious one, and carried to his home beyond the sea."

"And do you think there will be war?" asked a long-haired soldier, toying with the short dagger in his belt.

"How can it be otherwise?" answered the elder. "When Menelaus won peerless Helen for his wife, the noblest princes of Hellas promised with solemn oaths that they would aid him against anyone who should try either by guile or by force to take her from him. Let the word be carried from city to city, and all Hellas will soon be in arms. The king, with his brother Agamemnon, has even now crossed over to Pylos to take counsel with old Nestor, the wisest of men. When he comes back to Lacedæmon, you may expect to see the watch-fires blazing on the mountain-tops."

"No sight would be more welcome," answered the soldier.

"None, indeed, save only the towers and palaces of Troy in flames!" returned the other earnestly.

.   .   .   .

Meanwhile, with troubled brow and anxious heart, Menelaus sat in Nestor's halls, and told the story of his wrongs. Before him, seated on a fair embroidered couch, was the aged king, listening with eager ears. Behind him stood his brother Agamemnon, tall and strong, and with eye and forehead like mighty Zeus. Close by his feet two heroes sat: on this side, Antilochus, the valiant son of Nestor; and on that, sage Palamedes, prince of Eubœa's distant shores. The last had just arrived at Pylos, and had not learned the errand which had brought the king of Lacedæmon thither.

"Tell again the story of your visit to Troy," said Nestor. "Our guest, good Palamedes, would fain understand it all; and I doubt not that he may be of service to your cause."

Then Menelaus began once more at the beginning,—

"There is no need that I should speak of the long voyage to Ilios, or of the causes which per-suaded me to undertake it. When I drew near the lofty citadels of Troy, and through the Scæan gates could see the rows of stately dwellings and Athené's marble temple, and the busy market-place of that great city, I stopped there in wonder, fearing to venture farther. Then I sent a herald to the gates, who should make known my name and lineage, and the errand upon which I had come; but I waited without in the shade of a spreading beech, not far from the towering wall. Before me stood the mighty city; behind me the fertile plain sloped gently to the sea; in the distance I could see the tomb of Ilus and the sparkling waters of Scamander; while much farther, and on the other side, the wooded peak of Ida lifted itself toward the clouds. But I had not long to view this scene; for a noble company of men led by Paris himself, handsome as Apollo, came out of the gates to welcome me. With words of kind greeting from the king, they bade me enter within the walls. They led me through the Scæan gates and along the well-paved streets, until we came, at last, to Priam's noble hall. It was a splendid house, with broad doorways and polished porticos, and marble columns richly carved. Within were fifty chambers, joining one another, all walled with polished stone; in these abode the fifty sons of Priam with their wedded wives. On the other side, and opening into the court, were twelve chambers, built for his daughters; while over all were the sleeping-rooms for that noble household, and around were galleries and stairways leading to the king's great hall below.

"King Priam received me kindly, and, when he understood my errand, left naught undone to help me forward with my wishes. Ten days I abode as a guest in his halls, and when I would return to Lacedæmon, he pressed me to tarry yet a month in Troy. But the winds were fair, and the oracles promised a pleasant voyage, and I begged that on the twelfth day he would let me depart. So he and his sons brought many gifts, rich and beautiful, and laid them at my feet,—a fair mantle, and a doublet, and a talent of fine gold, and a sword with a silver-studded hilt, and a drinking-cup richly engraved that I might remember them when I pour libations to the gods.

" 'Take these gifts,' said Priam, 'as tokens of our friendship for you, and not only for you, but for all who dwell in distant Hellas. For we too are the children of the immortals. Our mighty ancestor, Dardanus, was the son of Zeus. He it was who built Dardania on the slopes of Ida, where the waters gush in many silvery streams from underneath the rocky earth. To Dardanus a son was born named Erichthonius, who, in his time, was the richest of mortal men. And Erichthonius was the father of Tros, to whom were born three noble sons, Ilus, Assaracus, and Ganymedes. The last was the handsomest of men, and for his beauty's sake the gods carried him to Ida's sacred summit to be the cup-bearer of Father Zeus and the companion of the immortals. Then Ilus had a son, famous in song and story, named Laomedon, who in his old age became my father. He, though my sire, did many unwise things, and brought sore distress upon the people of this land.

" 'One day Apollo and Poseidon came to sacred Troy, disguised as humble wayfarers seeking some employment. This they did because so ordered by mighty Zeus.

" ' "What can you do?" asked my father, when the two had told their wishes.

" 'Poseidon answered, "I am a builder of walls."

" 'And Apollo answered, "I am a shepherd, and a tender of herds."

" ' "It is well," answered Laomedon. "The wall-builder shall build a wall around this Troy so high and strong that no enemy can pass it. The shepherd shall tend my herds of crook-horned kine in the wooded glens of Ida. If at the end of a twelvemonth, the wall be built, and if the cattle thrive without loss of one, then I will pay you your hire: a talent of gold, two tripods of silver, rich robes, and armor such as heroes wear."

" 'So the shining archer, and the shaker of the earth, served my father through the year for the hire which he had promised. Poseidon built a wall, high and fair, around the city; and Apollo tended the shambling kine, and lost not one. But when they claimed their hire, Laomedon drove them away with threats, telling them that he would bind their feet and hands together, and sell them as slaves into some distant land, having first sheared off their ears with his sharp sword. And the twain went away with angry hearts, planning in their minds how they might avenge themselves.

" 'Back to his watery kingdom, and his golden palace beneath the sea, went great Poseidon. He harnessed his steeds to his chariot, and rode forth upon the waves. He loosed the mighty winds from their prison-house, and sent them raging over the sea. The angry waters rushed in upon the land; they covered the pastures and the rich plain of Troy, and threatened even to beat down the mighty walls which their king had built. Then, little by little, the flood shrank back again; and the people went out of the city to see the waste of slime and black mud which covered their meadows. While they were gazing upon the scene, a fearful monster, sent by angry Poseidon, came up out of the sea, and fell upon them, and drove them with hideous slaughter back to the city gates; neither would he allow any one to come outside of the walls.

" 'Then my father, in his great distress, clad himself in mourning, and went in deep humility to the temple of Athené, where stands the heaven-sent statue which we call Palladion. In sore distress, he called unto the goddess, and besought to know the means whereby the anger of Poseidon might be assuaged. And in solemn tones a voice came from the moveless lips of the Palladion, saying,—

" ' "Every day one of the maidens of Troy must be fed to the monster outside of the walls. The shaker of the earth has spoken. Disobey him not, lest more cruel punishments befall thee."

" 'Then in every house of Troy there was sore distress and lamentation, for no one knew upon whom the doom would soonest fall. And every day a hapless maiden, young and fair, was chained to the great rock by the shore, and left there to be the food of the pitiless monster. And the people cried aloud in their distress, and cursed the mighty walls and the high towers which had been reared by the unpaid labors of Poseidon; and my father sat upon his high seat, and trembled because of the dire calamities which his own deeds had brought upon his people.

" 'At last, after many humbler victims had perished, the lot fell upon the fairest of my sisters, Hesione, my father's best-loved daughter. In sorrow we arrayed her in garments befitting one doomed to an untimely death; and when we had bidden her a last farewell, we gave her to the heralds to lead forth to the place of sacrifice. Just then, however, a noble stranger, taller and more stately than any man in Troy, came down the street from the Scæan gate. Fair-haired and blue-eyed, handsome and strong, he seemed a very god to all who looked upon him. Over his shoulder he wore the tawny skin of a mighty lion, while in his hand he carried a club most wonderful to behold. And the people, as he passed, prayed him that he would free our city from the dread monster who was robbing us of our fair loved ones.

" ' "I know that thou art a god!" cried my father, when he saw the stranger. "I pray thee, save my daughter, who even now is being led forth to a cruel death!"

" ' "You make mistake," answered the fair stranger. "I am not one of the gods. My name is Heracles, and like you I am mortal. Yet I may help you in this your time of need."

" 'Now, in my father's stables there were twelve fair steeds, the best that the earth ever knew. So light of foot were they, that when they bounded over the land, they might run upon the topmost ears of ripened corn, and break them not; and when they bounded over the sea, not even Poseidon's steeds could glide so lightly upon the crests of the waves. Some say they were the steeds of Boreas given to my grandfather Tros, by his sire Erichthonius; others, that they were the price which Zeus paid for godlike Ganymedes, most beautiful of men. These steeds, my father promised to give to Heracles if he would save Hesione.

" 'Then the heralds led my fair sister to the shore, and chained her to the rock, there to wait for the coming of the monster. But Heracles stood near her, fearless in his strength. Soon the waves began to rise; the waters were disturbed, and the great beast, with hoarse bellowings, lifted his head above the breakers, and rushed forward to seize his fair prey. Then the hero sprang to meet him. With blow upon blow from his mighty club, he felled the monster; the waters of the sea were reddened with blood; Hesione was saved, and Troy was freed from the dreadful curse.

" ' "Behold thy daughter!" said Heracles, leading her gently back to the Scæan gate, and giving her to her father. "I have saved her from the jaws of death, and delivered your country from the dread scourge. Give me now my hire."

" 'Shame fills my heart as I tell this story, for thanklessness was the bane of my father's life. Ungrateful to the hero who had risked so much and done so much that our homes and our country might be saved from ruin, he turned coldly away

213

from Heracles; then he shut the great gates in his face, and barred him out of the city, and taunted him from the walls, saying, "I owe thee no hire! Begone from our coasts, ere I scourge thee hence!"

" 'Full of wrath, the hero turned away. "I go, but I will come again," he said.

" 'Then peace and plenty blessed once more the land of Ilios, and men forgot the perils from which they had been delivered. But ere long, great Heracles returned, as he had promised; and with him came a mighty fleet of white-sailed ships and many warriors. Neither gates nor strong walls could stand against him. Into the city he marched, and straight to my father's palace. All fled before him, and the strongest warriors quailed beneath his glance. Here, in this very court, he slew my father and my brothers with his terrible arrows. I myself would have fallen before his wrath, had not my sister, fair Hesione, pleaded for my life.

" ' "I spare his life," said Heracles, in answer to her prayers, "for he is but a lad. Yet he must be my slave until you have paid a price for him, and thus redeemed him."

" 'Then Hesione took the golden veil from her head, and gave it to the hero as my purchase price. And thenceforward I was called Priam, or the purchased; for the name which my mother gave me was Podarkes, or the fleet-footed.

" 'After this, Heracles and his heroes went on board their ships and sailed back across the sea, leaving me alone in my father's halls. For they took fair Hesione with them, and carried her to Salamis, to be the wife of Telamon, the sire of mighty Ajax. There, through these long years she has lived in sorrow, far removed from home and friends, and the scenes of her happy childhood. And now that the hero Telamon, to whom she was wedded, lives no longer, I ween that her life is indeed a cheerless one.'

"When Priam had finished his tale, he drew his seat still nearer mine, and looked into my face with anxious, beseeching eyes. Then he said, 'I have long wished to send a ship across the sea to bring my sister back to Troy. A dark-prowed vessel, built for speed and safety, lies now at anchor in the harbor, and a picked crew is ready to embark at any moment. And here is my son Paris, handsome and brave, who is anxious to make voyage to Salamis, to seek unhappy Hesione. Yet our seamen, having never ventured far from home, know nothing of the dangers of the deep, nor do they feel sure that they can find their way to Hellas. And so we have a favor to ask of you; and that is, that when your ship sails to-morrow, ours may follow in its wake across the sea.'

"I was glad when Priam spoke these words, for, in truth, I was loath to part with Paris; and I arranged at once that he should bear me company in my own swift ship, while his vessel with its crew followed not far behind.

"And so with favoring winds being blessed, we made voyage back to Lacedæmon, bringing with us the bones of my beloved countrymen. What followed is too sad for lengthy mention, and is in part already known to you. Need I tell you how I opened my halls to Paris, and left no courtesy undone that I might make him happy? Need I tell you how he was welcomed by fair Helen, and how the summer days fled by on golden wings; and how in the delights of Lacedæmon he forgot his errand to Salamis, and cared only to remain with me, my honored guest and trusted friend? One day a message came to me from my old friend Idomeneus. He had planned a hunt among the mountains and wooded vales of Crete, and he invited me to join him in the sport. I had not seen Idomeneus since the time that we together, in friendly contention, sought the hand of Helen. I could not do otherwise than accept his invitation, for he had sent his own ship to carry me over to Crete. So I bade farewell to Helen, saying, 'Let not our noble guest lack entertainment while I am gone; and may the golden hours glide happily until I come again.' And to Paris I said, 'Tarry another moon in Lacedæmon; and when I return from Crete, I will go with you to Salamis, and aid you in your search for Hesione.' Then I went on board the waiting ship, and prospering breezes carried us without delays to Crete.

"Idomeneus received me joyfully, and entertained me most royally in his palace; and for nine days we feasted in his halls, and made all things ready for the hunt. But, lo! on the evening of the last day, a vision came to me. Gold-winged Iris, the fleet-footed messenger of the gods, stood before me.

'Hasten back to Lacedæmon,' she cried, 'for thou art robbed of thy dearest treasure!' And even while she spoke, one of my own ships came sailing into the harbor, bringing trusted heralds whom the elders of Lacedæmon had sent to me. They told me the fatal news. 'No sooner were you well on your way,' they said, 'than Paris began to put his ship in readiness to depart. Helen prayed him to tarry until your return, but he would not hearken. "I will stay no longer," he said. "My seamen rest upon their oars; the sails of my ship are spread; the breeze will soon spring up that will carry me to my own fair home across the sea. But you, beauteous Helen, shall go with me; for the deathless gods have spoken it. Aphrodite, long ago, promised that the most beautiful woman in the world should be my wife. And who is that most beautiful woman if it is not yourself? Come! fly over the sea, and be my queen. It is the will of the gods." '

"It was thus that the perfidious Trojan wrought the ruin of all that was dear to me. At first, Helen refused. But Paris is a handsome prince, and day after day he renewed his suit. Then on the sixth day she yielded. In the darkness of the night they went on board his waiting vessel, carrying with them the gold and jewels of my treasure-house; and in the morning, when the sun arose on Lacedæmon, they were far out at sea.

"You know the rest: how in wrath and great sorrow I hurried home from Crete; how I first counselled with my own elders, and then with my brother Agamemnon of Mycenæ. And now, O noble

Nestor, we have come to Pylos, seeking thy advice. On these two things my mind is set: Helen must be mine again, and Paris must suffer the punishment due to traitors."

When Menelaus had ended, sage Nestor answered with many words of counsel. "Keep the thought of vengeance ever before you," he said. "Yet act not rashly. The power of Troy is very great; and, in case of war, all the tribes of Asia will make common cause with Ilios. But an insult to Lacedæmon is an insult to all Hellas, and every loyal Hellene will hasten to avenge it. More than this, the chiefs of almost every state have already sworn to aid you. We have but to call upon them, and remind them of their oaths, and all the mightiest warriors of our land will take up arms against the power of Troy."

Then Palamedes spoke in like manner, and his words had great weight with Menelaus; for among all the heroes there were few who equalled him in wisdom. He it was who first built beacon fires on the headlands and light houses to warn venturous seamen of the hidden dangers in their way; he it was who first invented scales for weighing, and who taught men how to measure grain and wine by certain standards; he it was who first made dice, and who showed what beauty and mystery lie hidden in the letters which Cadmus brought from Phœnicia to Hellas. And he was wise in state-craft and the knowledge of human nature.

"Nestor has spoken well," he said, addressing Menelaus, "and it behooves us to follow his advice. Now do you and Agamemnon return at once to Argos and Lacedæmon, and call upon the fighting men along the eastern coast to join you in the war. In the mean while, Nestor and myself will do the same, here on the western coast and among the islands of the sea."

"By the way," said Nestor, "there is Odysseus, king of Ithaca,—the rarest and bravest of men. Did he but know of this affair, he would be a host within himself, to lead us to sure victory."

"That is true," said Palamedes, "and we must seek his aid first. My ship lies now at anchor, just off the beach; and if noble Nestor will be my comrade, we will sail to-morrow to Ithaca, and make sure of his valued aid."

"Most surely I will go with you," said old Nestor. "And I will never rest nor give up the fight, until Helen is returned to Menelaus, and Paris has received his due reward."

ADVENTURE XVIII

AN UNWILLING HERO

In the shade of the orchard trees, at the foot of Mount Neritus, there was gathered, one afternoon, a happy family party. The chief figure in the group was white-haired Laertes, in his gardener's garb, picking some ripe fruit from the overloaded branches. At his right stood Anticleia, as queenly beautiful as when her hero-husband had won her in the halls of old Autolycus. At his left was Penelope, her sweet face beaming with smiles; while on the ground beside her sat Odysseus, gently dandling in his arms the babe Telemachus, and laughing at the budding wisdom of the child.

"Some men wander the wide world over, seeking for empty glory," said he, turning towards Penelope. "But I would rather have my pleasant home, and live amid its never-failing delights, than share the honors even of great Heracles."

At this moment, Phemius the bard was seen coming in haste from the palace. "What news, Phemius?" asked Odysseus. "Hast thou finished that new song of thine? And dost thou hasten thus to sing it to us before some part of it shall go out of thy mind?"

"Nay, master," answered the bard, speaking in anxious tones. "I have come to tell you that there are guests waiting in the hall. Famous men they are,—even Nestor, king of Pylos, and shrewd Palamedes of Eubœa. And they bring wonderful news,—news of that which will, perchance, fill our land with sadness."

"Tell me what it is," said Odysseus.

Then the bard told the story of Paris and Helen, as he had learned it briefly from Palamedes; and he explained the errand of the hero-guests which they had thoughtlessly imparted to him. Odysseus looked at his smiling babe, and at his fair wife, and his loved mother, and his honored father; and his brow darkened as he shook his head, and said, "Why should I risk so much, and, joining in this war, leave all that is dear to me on earth, simply for the sake of Menelaus and his misguided Helen?"

Then, after a moment's thought, he added, "I will not go. Tell Nestor and Palamedes that I am mad, and cannot go."

All at once a great change seemed to come over him. He put the babe into its nurse's arms; and then with long strides, and in the aimless manner of a maniac, he made his way across the orchard, and along the foot-path by the beach to the white palace near the shore. When his old friends, Nestor and

Palamedes, saw him, they hastened towards him, expecting to receive his greeting; but with unmeaning words, and a vacant stare, he passed by them without a word of recognition.

"He is mad," said the frightened servants, as they fled before him.

"Yes, he is mad, and knows not where he is nor what he does," said Phemius, hastily rejoining the guests. "When I went out to find him just now, he was wandering among the fruit trees, picking the green fruit, and roaring like a wild beast. The gods have taken his reason from him."

"How sad that so great a mind should be thus clouded!" answered Nestor, with a sigh. "And at this time it is doubly sad for us and for all who love him, for we had counted on great things from shrewd Odysseus. Surely some unfriendly god has done this thing with intent to harm all Hellas."

"Do not judge hastily," whispered Palamedes. "We shall find out from whence this madness comes."

Soon Odysseus rushed from his chamber, looking wildly about him, as if the very Furies were at his heels. He was dressed in his richest garments, and on his shoulder he carried a bag of salt. Without speaking to any one, he made his way to the stables, where, with his own hands, he harnessed a mule and a cow, and yoked them side by side to a plough. Then he drove his strange team down to the beach, and he began to plough long, deep furrows in the sand. By and by, he opened the bag of salt, and strewed the grains here and there, as though he were sowing seed. This strange work he continued until the daylight faded into darkness, and all the people were fain to seek rest under their home-roofs. Then he drove his team back to the stables, unyoked the beasts and fed them, and hurried silently to his chamber.

The next morning, as soon as the dawn appeared, he was seen ploughing the sandy beach as before.

"I will see whether there be any reason in his madness," said Palamedes to Nestor.

It chanced at that moment, that Eurycleia the nurse was passing by with little Telemachus in her arms. Without another word, Palamedes lifted the babe, and laid it smiling in the last furrow that Odysseus had made, so that on his next round the team would trample upon it. As Odysseus drew near, urging forward the mule and the cow, with many cries and maniacal gestures, he saw the helpless babe. The sight of its danger made him forget himself and his assumed madness; he turned his team aside, and running forward seized Telemachus, and, kissing his laughing lips, handed him, with every show of gentleness, to the good nurse.

"Ha, Odysseus!" cried Palamedes. "Thou canst not deceive us. Thou art no more mad than I am. Cease now that boyish play, and come and talk with us as becometh a hero."

Then Odysseus, seeing that he had been fairly outwitted by one as shrewd as himself, knew that further pretence of madness would avail him nothing. For a single moment his brow was clouded with anger, and he whispered hoarsely to Palamedes, "You shall have your reward for this!" Then, leaving his plough and his ill-matched team upon the beach, he took his two guests kindly by the hand, and led them into his palace. A great feast was spread upon the tables, and the morning was spent in eating and merry-making, and not a word was said concerning the great business which had brought the kings to Ithaca.

Later in the day, however, Nestor told Odysseus the story of the perfidy of Paris. Then Palamedes followed with a speech so clear, so forcible, that the hearts of all who heard it were stirred to their very depths; and Odysseus, rising from his seat, renewed the vow which he had made when Menelaus won fair Helen for his bride. And from that time to the very end, there was not a man among all the Hellenes, who threw himself more earnestly into the work than did Odysseus.

For seven days Nestor and Palamedes tarried at Ithaca, talking with Odysseus, and making plans for the war against Troy. On the eighth day, the three heroes embarked for the mainland; and for months they journeyed from country to country, and from city to city, reminding the princes of their vows, and stirring all Hellas into a flame. Soon the watch-fires were kindled on every mountain-top; and every warrior in the land made haste to see that his arms were in order, and every seaman to put his ship to rights. And Ares, the mighty god of battle, brandished his sword above the sea; dread comets blazed red in mid-heaven; glittering stars fell to the earth, or shot gleaming athwart the sky. Sounds of warlike preparation were heard, not only in the dwellings of men, but even in the halls of Zeus, upon the airy summit of Olympus.

ADVENTURE XIX

HEROES IN STRANGE GARB

THERE dwelt at Mycenæ a wise soothsayer, named Calchas,—a man versed in all the lore of earth and sky, and holding some sort of communion with the immortals. He could lift the veil of the future, and see what to other men lay hidden in the darkness; and next to the Pythian oracle at Delphi, or the talking oak of Dodona, he was held in high repute as knowing the counsels of the gods. When all the great chiefs sat one day in Agamemnon's hall, and talked of their warriors and their ships and their arms, and boasted of their readiness to sail at once for Ilios, the old soothsayer came and stood before them. His white locks streamed in flowing waves about his shoulders; his gray eyes gleamed with a strange, wild light; he moved his long arms to and fro above his head, and pointed with his thin fingers first towards the sky, and then towards the sea.

"Hearken ye to the seer," said Menelaus; "he has had a vision, and perchance he can tell us how we shall fare in this great business which we have undertaken."

Then Calchas spoke and said, "Verily I know not any thing of this matter, save by the gift of soothsaying which the far-darting Apollo has bestowed upon me. Yet when I inquired of him, this answer did he give: 'Let the long haired Hellenes make war upon Troy. They shall not prevail against that city unless Achilles, the dear son of Thetis, lead them.' Send now for him, and enlist him in your cause; for otherwise you shall fail, and the Trojans shall boast of your ruin!"

Having said these words, the seer strode from the hall, leaving the hero chiefs alone. For a time they sat in silence, each pondering the matter in his own mind. Then Agamemnon spoke, and his words were full of anger and unbelief. "Never yet," said he, "did Calchas prophesy any thing but ill. He sees naught but evil; and when we feel most sure of success, then it is the joy of his heart to foretell failure. Now, after the gods have thus far favored us, and when all things are in readiness for the gathering together of our forces, this woful soothsayer comes to tell us that without Achilles we shall fail. For my part, I care little for his words, and am willing to run all risks."

"Say not so," quickly answered Odysseus. "The old man speaks as Apollo gives him utterance; and no man shall dare put his judgment in the scales against the foreknowledge of the gods. Let us seek Achilles at once, and persuade him to join us in our league against Ilios."

"But who shall find him?" asked Menelaus. "Two months ago, I was in Iolcos by the sea, whither I had gone to see old Peleus. I found that that aged king dwelt no longer in the ancient city, but had removed into his own country of Phthia, and there abode among his Myrmidons. Into Phthia, therefore, I went, hoping to find Achilles also there. But old Peleus wept when I asked about his son. 'In truth, I know not where the young man is,' he said, in answer to my questions. 'For when the news was noised about, that the chiefs of Hellas were planning war upon Troy, then silver-footed Thetis carried her son into some distant, unknown land, and hid him there. For the Fates have declared the doom of Achilles, that his days on earth shall be few but glorious; and his mother feared, that, should he join in the great war, he would meet an untimely death. Thus, then, it is that I am bereft already of my only son; for I know not whether I shall ever again behold him.' In this manner Peleus, the lord of horses, bewailed the absence of his son. And though in every city I sought news concerning the whereabouts of the young hero, I could learn nothing whatever. Even Patroclus, his bosom friend and comrade, wept for him as for one dead. I do not believe that he can be found in Hellas."

Then Nestor the wise arose and spoke. "It does not become us," he said, "to doubt or dispute the words of Calchas the seer. Therefore we must find Achilles, and win him to our cause; or, laying aside all thought of war, we must humbly surrender to Paris the noblest treasure of our country, even beauteous Helen."

"Achilles can be found," said Odysseus. "I myself will seek him, and the moon shall not wane thrice ere I shall have found him. Let the best ship in Argos be put in readiness at once; and let a crew of the most skilful oarsmen be chosen, and a good store of food be put into the hold. I will embark to-morrow, and you shall see me no more until I bring good news of Thetis's godlike son."

So then Odysseus set sail on a long, uncertain voyage to the islands of the sea, in search of the hidden hero. Vainly did he visit Cythera, the lofty isle where Aphrodite first rose in all her beauty from the salt sea-foam; he touched at Melos, rich in corn and wine; he skirted Paros, known to all the world for its figs and its spotless marble; he stopped for a month at sacred Delos, the birthplace of Apollo; he explored well-watered Ophiussa, where serpents curse the ground, and grapes grow purple on the climbing vines; he sought long time in Andros among the groves and in the temple sacred to ruddy-faced Dionysus: yet in none of these lands heard he any news of the godlike son of Peleus. Weary of their long and fruitless voyage, the comrades of Odysseus murmured sorely, and besought him to return to Mycenæ, and give up the search. But he turned a deaf ear to their pleadings, and sailed away to Scyros, where old Lycomedes reigned. For the bright-eyed goddess Athené had whispered to him in a dream, and told him that in the court of Lycomedes he would find the hero for whom he sought.

In a narrow inlet, hidden by trees and tall reeds, the ship was moored, while shrewd Odysseus went alone and unheralded to the palace of the king. He had laid aside his warrior's gear, and was now attired in the guise of a wandering peddler, and loaded with a heavy pack of precious wares. And lo! as he neared the high-built halls of Lycomedes, he came to a spacious garden just outside of the courtyard, and hard by the lofty gate. A green hedge ran round it on four sides, while within grew many tall trees laden with fruits and blossoms,—pear trees, pomegranates, apple trees, and olives. So well cared for were these trees, that they yielded fruit in every season of the year, nor ever failed, even in winter time. Beyond these, all manner of garden-beds were planted, where flowers bloomed in never-ending freshness,—the dewy lotus, the crocus flower, the pale hyacinth, violets, asphodels, and fair lilies. And in their midst, two springs of never-failing water gushed: one of them watered the garden and the fields beyond; the other ran close by the threshold of the palace, and bubbled up in the market-square, where all the people came to fill their vessels.

As Odysseus stood and gazed in rapt delight upon this scene of beauty, a party of happy maidens came through the courtyard, and stopped in the garden to pluck the fruits and flowers. Then on the open lawn, they fell to playing ball; and one among them sang a lightsome song as they tossed the missile to and fro, or danced with happy feet upon the smooth-mown sward. When they saw Odysseus standing in the path, they stopped their game, and stood silent in their places, scarce knowing whether to advance and greet the stranger kindly, or in girlish timidness to flee into the palace. The hero opened then his peddler's pack, and held up to their delighted gaze a golden necklace set with amber beads. No further thought of flight had the maidens now. With eager yet hesitating feet, they came crowding around him, anxious to see what other thing of beauty he had brought with him. One by one, he showed them all his treasures,—ear-rings, bracelets of finest workmanship, clasps, buckles, head-bands, and golden hair-pins. These they took in their hands, and, passing them from one to another, eagerly debated the price. One only of the company, taller and nobler than the others, stood aloof, and seemed to care nothing for the rich and handsome ornaments. Odysseus noticed this, but shrewdly kept his counsels to himself.

"A merchant like myself," said he, "must needs have goods for all,—for the young as well as for the old, for the grave as well as for the gay, for the hero as well as for the lady. It is his duty no less than his delight to please."

With these words he laid before the maidens a sword with hilt most deftly carved, a dagger with long keen blade, and a helmet thickly inlaid with precious gems. The one who had not cared to look at the trinkets now started quickly as if a trumpet had blown; she took up the sword, and handled it like a warrior long used to weapons; she tested the edge of the dagger, and sounded the strength of the helmet. Odysseus had learned all that he wished to know. He thought no more of the ornaments,—the bracelets, the clasps, and the hair-pins,—but gave them to the maidens for any price that they chose to offer. When all were pleased and satisfied, he turned to that one still toying with the sword, and said sharply,—

"Achilles!"

Had an earthquake shaken the isle of Scyros at that moment, Achilles would not have been more startled. For the tall, fair body, clad in a maiden's robes, was none other than that long-sought hero.

"Achilles," again said Odysseus, "I know thee, and it is useless to struggle longer against thy destiny. Put off that unbecoming garb, and come with me. Thy countrymen need thee to aid them in waging bitter war against Troy."

Then he told to the listening hero the story of the great wrong which Paris had done,—the unbearable insult which he had put upon the folk of Hellas. No man ever used words more persuasive. When he had ended, Achilles took him by the hand, and said, "Odysseus, truly do I know the destiny which is mine, and it behooves no man to struggle long against the doom which has been allotted to him. For the gods ordain that man should live in pain, while they themselves are sorrowless. You have heard it said, how on the threshold of Zeus there stand two caskets full of gifts to men. One casket holds the evil, and one the good; and to whomsoever is dealt a mingled lot, upon him misfortunes sometimes fall, and sometimes blessings. So it is with me and with my father's house. For upon Peleus were bestowed rich gifts, even from his birth, and he excelled all other men in good fortune and in wealth; and he was king over the Myrmidons; and to him was given a sea-nymph for a wife, even Thetis, my goddess-mother. Yet, with all the good, sorrow has come upon him in his old age; for in his halls there are no kingly sons to gladden his heart, and hold up his hands. I am his only son, and of me it has been written that I am doomed to an untimely death; and it was for this that silver-footed Thetis brought me hither across the sea, and, clothing me in maidenly attire, left me to serve in Lycomedes' pleasant halls. But I tire of life like this. I would rather die to-morrow, a hero in some grand struggle, than live a hundred years among these soft delights. I will sail with you at once for Phthia, where my father sits, already bereaved, in his spacious halls. There I will summon my Myrmidons, and my best-loved friend Patroclus; and then with eager hearts we will hasten to join our countrymen in war against the Trojan power."

. . . .

Thus, then, did Odysseus perform his quest, and thus the last and greatest ally was won to the Hellenic cause. And yet the war was long delayed. Many times did the moon wax and wane; and seed-time and harvest, and fruit-gathering, and the storms of winter, came again and again in their turn,—and still the heroes were unready to join their forces and enter upon the mighty struggle.

At length, however, after nearly ten years had passed, all the princes and warriors of Hellas gathered their ships and men together at Aulis, and along the shores of the Euripus. A thousand dark-hulled vessels were moored in the strait; and a hundred thousand brave men were on board, ready to follow their leaders whithersoever they should order.

Chief of all that host was mighty Agamemnon, king of men, bearing the sceptre of Mycenæ, which Hephaestus, long before, had wrought most wondrously. He was clad in flashing armor, and his mind was filled with overweening pride when he thought how high he stood among the warriors, and that his men were the goodliest and bravest of all that host.

Next to him was Menelaus, silent and discreet, by no means skilled above his fellows, and yet, by reason of his noble heart, beloved and honored by all the Greeks; and it was to avenge his wrongs that this mighty array of men and ships had been gathered together.

Odysseus came next, shrewd in counsels, and no longer an unwilling hero; but, earnest and active, he moved among the men and ships, inspiring all with zeal and courage. He wore upon his shoulders a thick purple mantle, clasped with a golden brooch of curious workmanship, which Penelope had given to him as a parting gift. Around his waist was a shining tunic, soft and smooth, and bright as the sunshine. With him, wherever he went, was his herald and armor-bearer, Eurybates,—a hunchbacked, brown-skinned, curly-haired man, whom Odysseus held in high esteem because of his rare good sense.

There, also, was young Achilles, tall and handsome, and swift of foot. His long hair fell about his shoulders like a shower of gold, and his gray eyes gleamed like those of the mountain eagle. By the shore lay his trim ships—fifty in all—with thousands of gallant Myrmidons on board. And ever at his side was his bosom friend and comrade, Patroclus, the son of Menoitios. He it was to whom old Peleus had said when they were about embarking for Aulis, "Thou art older than my child Achilles, but he is nobler born and mightier far in warlike deeds. But thou art wise and prudent; therefore, do thou speak gentle words of warning to him, and show him what is best to do: he will hearken to thy words spoken for his good."

There also was Ajax, the valiant son of Telamon, huge in body and slow in speech, but, next to Achilles, the bravest of all the host. And the other Ajax, clad in his linen corslet, and master of forty ships from Locris, moved also among the mightiest of the heroes.

There, too, was Nestor, the aged king of Pylos, rich in wisdom and experience, and skilled in persuasive speech. With him was his son Antilochus,

235

the quondam suitor of fair Helen, a warrior worthy of such a sire.

And there was Idomeneus, the stalwart chief who ruled the hundred cities of Crete, and was the sworn friend of Menelaus. And there was Philoctetes, the cunning archer, carrying the great bow which had been given him for his last sad act of friendship to his master, Heracles. And there was Diomede, of the loud war-cry, wearing the skin of a great fiery lion round his shoulders, and marshalling the warriors who had come with him from Argos, and Tiryns of the mighty walls. And there, too, among so many others of far greater worth, was Nireus of Syma, his well-oiled locks as neatly curled, and his linen as spotlessly white, as when in youth he had sued for Helen's hand in the court of old Tyndareus.

Now when the day had come for the fleet to sail, the chiefs stood upon the shore, and offered solemn sacrifices to Poseidon, and prayed the gods to prosper them in their undertaking and bring them safe again to their loved homes in Hellas. While they were burning the choicest bits of fat and flesh, behold, a strange thing happened! From a crevice in the rocks a shining serpent, with glittering cold eyes and forked tongue, came creeping silently into the sunlight. The heroes gazed upon it with wonder in their faces, for they knew that it was sent as a sign to them. Not far away stood a plane-tree, green with foliage, in which a bird had built her nest; and in the nest were nine tiny fledglings, tenderly cared for by the mother bird. Straight to this tree the serpent crept; it twined around the trunk, and stealthily climbed to the nest; it seized the helpless little ones in its fangs, and devoured them; then it darted upon the distressed mother bird, and destroyed her most pitilessly. But now a gleam of lightning flashed across the sky, and a peal of thunder shook the earth and sea. When the astonished chiefs looked up again, behold, the serpent had been turned into stone.

"Call Calchas the seer, and let him tell us what this portends!" they cried.

Then Calchas, his long hair streaming in the wind, his wild eyes rolling in awe, his gaunt arms waving to and fro above his head, came and looked upon the wonder.

"Ye men of Hellas!" he cried, "I will tell you what this portends. As there were nine birds in the nest, ye shall war nine years against Troy, and shall not prevail; but, even as the serpent destroyed the mother bird, so in the tenth year shall the city and its god-built walls fall into your hands."

BECALMED AT AULIS

A PLEASANT wind from the west sprang up, and drove the great fleet out into the sea. Not a single one of the thousand ships was lost or left behind; and after a quick and happy voyage, they came in sight of a fruitful land and a great city with high towers and pleasant dwellings.

"The gods have favored us, even beyond what we asked!" cried the Hellenes.

Achilles and his Myrmidons landed first, and without waiting for the other ships to come up, they rushed across the plain, and began an assault upon the town. Like a swarm of locusts lighting down upon a field of grain, and consuming every thing before them, so came the destroying Hellenes. The gates were broken down; the astonished people fled in dismay, and sought safety among the hills and in the forest on the other side of the town. Not until many houses had been burned, and many people slain, did Odysseus and Menelaus, whose ships had been delayed, reach the place.

"Men of Hellas!" they cried, hastening into the midst of the carnage. "What is this you are doing? This is not Troy. It is the peaceful city of Teuthrania in Mysia. Cease your slaughter, and return at once to your vessels, lest the wrath of the gods fall upon you."

The word was carried from mouth to mouth; and the hasty heroes, crestfallen and ashamed, stopped their bloody work, and turned their faces back towards the shore where their ships lay beached. None too soon did they retreat; for the king of Mysia, one Telephus a son of Heracles, having quickly called his warriors together, fell upon their rear, and slew great numbers of them, following them even to the sloping beach. As the last ship was pushing out, an arrow from the bow of King Telephus struck Patroclus, wounding him sorely. Then Achilles, poising his long spear, threw it with deadly aim among the Mysians; it struck King Telephus, and laid him senseless though not slain upon the sandy plain.

No sooner had the fleet set sail again upon the sea, than Poseidon stirred up the waves in anger, and loosed the winds upon them. Great was the terror, and great indeed was the destruction. Some of the ships were sunk in mid-sea, and some were driven upon the rocks and wrecked. But the greater number of them, after days and weeks of buffeting with the waves, made their way back to Aulis.

When the heroes stood again on the shores of the Euripus, they began to think that doubtless there was some truth in the omen of the snake and the birds; and the most hopeful among them ceased to dream of taking Troy in a day. While waiting for stragglers to come in, and for the shattered vessels to be repaired, they found enough to do to keep the time from dragging heavily; and when not engaged in some kind of labor they amused themselves with various games, and great sport had they with quoits and javelins, with bows and arrows, and in wrestling and running. And now and then they went out into the woods of Eubœa, and hunted the wild deer which roamed there in abundance.

One day it chanced that Agamemnon, while hunting, started a fine stag, and gave it a long chase among the hills, and through the wooded dells, until it sought safety in a grove sacred to Artemis the huntress queen. The proud king knew that this was a holy place where beasts and birds might rest secure from harm; yet he cared naught for what Artemis had ordained, and with his swift arrows he slew the panting deer. Then was the huntress queen moved with anger, and she declared that the ships of the Hellenes should not sail from Aulis until the king had atoned for his crime. And a great calm rested upon the sea, and not a breath of air stirred the sails at the mast-heads of the ships. Day after day and week after week went by, and not a speck of cloud was seen in the sky above, and not a ripple on the glassy face of the deep. All the ships had been put in order, new vessels had been built, the warriors had burnished their armor and overhauled their arms a thousand times; and yet no breeze arose to waft them across the sea. And they began to murmur, and to talk bitterly against Agamemnon and the chiefs.

In the mean while, a small vessel driven by rowers came up the Euripus, and stopped among the ships at Aulis. On board of it was King Telephus of Mysia, sorely suffering from the wound which Achilles had given him on the Teuthranian beach. He had come to seek the hero who had wounded him, for an oracle had told him that he only could heal the grievous hurt. Achilles carried the sufferer to his tent, and skilfully dressed the wound, and bound it up with healing herbs; for in his boyhood he had learned from wise old Cheiron how to treat such ailments, and now that knowledge was of great use to him. And soon the king was whole and strong again; and he vowed that he would not leave Achilles, but would stay with the Hellenes, and pilot them across the sea to Troy. Yet the wrath of Artemis continued, and not the slightest breeze arose to cool the air, or fill the waiting sails of the ships.

At last Agamemnon sent for Calchas the soothsayer, and asked him in secret how the anger of the huntress queen might be assuaged. And the soothsayer with tears and lamentations answered that in no wise could it be done save by the sacrifice to Artemis of his maiden daughter Iphigenia. Then the king cried aloud in his grief, and declared that though Troy might stand forever, he would not do that thing; and he bade a herald go through the camp, and among the ships, and bid every man depart as he chose to his own country. But before the herald had gone from his tent, behold his brother Menelaus, the wronged husband of fair Helen, stood before him with downcast eyes and saddest of hearts.

"After ten years of labor and hope," said he to Agamemnon, "wouldst thou give up this enterprise, and lose all?"

Then Odysseus came also into the tent, and added his persuasions to those of Menelaus. And the king hearkened to him, for no man was more crafty in counsel; and the three recalled the herald, and formed a plan whereby they might please Artemis by doing as she desired. And Agamemnon, in his weakness, wrote a letter to Clytemnestra his queen, telling her to bring the maiden Iphigenia to Aulis, there to be wedded to King Achilles. *"Fail not in this,"* added he, *"for the godlike hero will not sail with us unless my daughter is given to him in marriage."* And when he had written the letter, he sealed it, and sent it by a swift messenger to Clytemnestra at Mycenæ.

Nevertheless the king's heart was full of sorrow, and when he was alone he planned how he might yet save his daughter. Night came, but he could not sleep; he walked the floor of his tent; he wept and lamented like one bereft of reason. At length he sat down, and wrote another letter: *"Daughter of Leda, send not thy child to Aulis, for I will give her in marriage at another time."* Then he called another messenger, an old and trusted servant of the household, and put this letter into his hands.

"Take this with all haste to my queen, who, perchance, is even now on her way to Aulis. Stop not by any cool spring in the groves, and let not thine eyes close for sleep. And see that the chariot bearing the queen and Iphigenia pass thee not unnoticed."

The messenger took the letter, and hasted away. But hardly had he passed the line of the tents when Menelaus saw him, and took the letter from him. And when he had read it, he went before his brother, and reproached him with bitter words.

"Before you were chosen captain of the host," said he, "you were kind and gentle, and the friend of every man. There was nothing that you would not do to aid your fellows. Now you are puffed up with pride and vain conceit, and care nothing even for those who are your equals in power. Yet, for all, you are not rid of your well-known cowardice; and when you saw that your leadership was likely to be taken away from you unless you obeyed the commands of Artemis, you agreed to do this thing. Now you are trying to break your word, sending secretly to your wife, and bidding her not to bring her daughter to Aulis."

Then Agamemnon answered, "Why should I destroy my daughter in order to win back thy wife? Let the suitors who swore an oath to King Tyndareus go with thee. In what way am I bound to serve thee?"

"Do as you will," said Menelaus, going away in wrath.

Soon after this, there came a herald to the king, saying, "Behold, your daughter Iphigenia has come as you directed, and with her mother and her little brother Orestes she rests by the spring close to the outer line of tents. And the warriors have gathered around them, and are praising her loveliness, and asking many questions; and some say, 'The king is sick to see his daughter whom he loves so deeply, and he has made up some excuse to bring her to the camp.' But I know why you have brought her here; for I have been told about the wedding, and the noble groom who is to lead her in marriage; and we will rejoice and be glad, because this is a happy day for the maiden."

Then the king was sorely distressed, and knew not what to do. "Sad, sad indeed," said he, "is the wedding to which the maiden cometh. For the name of the bridegroom is Death."

At the same time Menelaus came back, sorrowful and repentant. "You were right, my brother," said he. "What, indeed, has Iphigenia to do with Helen, and why should the maiden die for me? Send the Hellenes to their homes, and let not this great wrong be done."

"But how can I do that now?" asked Agamemnon. "The warriors, urged on by Odysseus and Calchas, will force me to do the deed. Or, if I flee to Mycenæ, they will follow me, and slay me, and destroy my city. Oh, woe am I, that such a day should ever dawn upon my sight!"

Even while they spoke together, the queen's chariot drove up to the tent's door, and the queen and Iphigenia and the little Orestes alighted quickly, and merrily greeted the king.

"It is well that you have sent for me, my father," said Iphigenia, caressing him.

"It may be well, and yet it may not," said Agamemnon. "I am exceeding glad to see thee alive and happy."

"If you are glad, why then do you weep?"

"I am sad because thou wilt be so long time away from me."

"Are you going on a very long voyage, father?"

"A long voyage and a sad one, my child. And thou, also, hast a journey to make."

"Must I make it alone, or will my mother go with me?"

"Thou must make it alone. Neither father nor mother nor any friend can go with thee, my child."

"But when shall it be? I pray that you will hasten this matter with Troy, and return home ere then."

"It may be so. But I must offer a sacrifice to the gods, before we sail from Aulis."

"That is well. And may I be present?"

"Yes, and thou shalt be very close to the altar."

"Shall I lead in the dances, father?"

Then the king could say no more, for reason of the great sorrow within him; and he kissed the maiden, and sent her into the tent. A little while afterward, the queen came and spoke to him, and asked him about the man to whom their daughter was to be wedded; and Agamemnon, still dissembling, told her that the hero's name was Achilles, and that he was the son of old Peleus and the sea-nymph Thetis.

"And when and where is the marriage to be?" asked the queen.

"On the first lucky day in the present moon, and here in our camp at Aulis," answered Agamemnon.

"Shall I stay here with thee until then?"

"Nay, thou must go back to Mycenæ without delay."

"But may I not come again? If I am not here, who will hold up the torch for the bride?"

"I will attend to all such matters," answered Agamemnon.

But Clytemnestra was not well pleased, neither could the king persuade her at all that she should return to Mycenæ. While yet they were talking, Achilles himself came to the tent door, and said aloud to the servant who kept it, "Tell thy master that Achilles, the son of Peleus, would be pleased to see him."

When Clytemnestra overheard these words, she hastened to the door, and offered the hero her hand. But he was ashamed and drew back, for it was deemed an unseemly thing for men to speak thus with women. Then Clytemnestra said, "Why, indeed, should you, who are about to marry my daughter, be ashamed to give me your hand?"

Achilles was struck with wonder, and asked her what she meant; and when she had explained the matter, he said,—

"Truly I have never been a suitor for thy daughter, neither has Agamemnon or Menelaus spoken a word to me regarding her."

And now the queen was astonished in her turn, and cried out with shame that she had been so cruelly deceived. Then the keeper of the door, who was the same that had been sent with the letter, came forward and told the truth regarding the whole matter. And Clytemnestra cried to Achilles, "O son of the silver-footed Thetis! Help me and help my daughter Iphigenia, in this time of sorest need! For we have no friend in all this host, and none in whom we can confide but thee."

Achilles answered, "Long time ago I was a pupil of old Cheiron the most righteous of men, and from him I learned to be honest and true. If

Agamemnon rule according to right, then I will obey him; but not otherwise. And now since thy daughter was brought to this place under pretence of giving her to me as my bride, I will see that she shall not be slain, neither shall any one dare take her from me."

On the following day, while Agamemnon sat grief-stricken in his tent, the maiden came before him carrying the babe Orestes in her arms; and she cast herself upon her knees at his feet, and caressing his hands, she thus besought him: "Would, dear father, that I had the voice of Orpheus, to whom even the rocks did listen! then I would persuade thee. O father! I am thy child. I was the first to call thee 'Father,' and the first to whom thou saidst 'My child.'"

The father turned his face away, and wept; he could not speak for sadness. Then the maiden went on: "O, father, hear me! thou to whom my voice was once so sweet that thou wouldst waken me to hear my prattle amid the songs of birds when it was meaningless as theirs. And when I was older grown, then thou wouldst say to me, 'Some day, my birdling, thou shalt have a nest of thy own, a home of which thou shalt be the mistress.' And I did answer, 'Yes, dear father, and when thou art old I will care for thee, and pay thee with all my heart for the kindness thou dost show me.' But now thou hast forgotten it all, and art ready to slay my young life."

A deep groan burst from the lips of the mighty king, but he spoke not a word. Then after a death-like silence broken only by the deep breathings of father and child, Iphigenia spoke again: "My father, can there be any prayer more pure and more persuasive than that of a maiden for her father's welfare? and when the cruel knife shall strike me down, thou wilt have one daughter less to pray for thee." A shudder shook the frame of Agamemnon, but he answered not a word.

At that moment Achilles entered. He had come in haste from the tents beside the shore, and he spoke in hurried, anxious accents.

"Behold," said he, "a great tumult has arisen in the camp; for Calchas has given out among the men that you refuse to do what Artemis has bidden, and that hence these delays and troubles have arisen. And the rude soldiers are crying out against you, and declaring that the maiden must die. When I would have stayed their anger, they took up stones to stone me,—my own Myrmidons among the rest. And now they are making ready to move upon your tent, threatening to sacrifice you also with your daughter. But I will fight for you to the utmost, and the maiden shall not die."

As he was speaking, Calchas entered, and, grasping the wrist of the pleading maiden, lifted her to her feet. She looked up, and saw his stony face and hard cold eyes; and turning again to Agamemnon, she said, "O father, the ships shall sail, for I will die for thee."

Then Achilles said to her, "Fair maiden, thou art by far the noblest and most lovely of thy sex.

Fain would I save thee from this fate, even though every man in Hellas be against me. Fly with me quickly to my long-oared galley, and I will carry thee safely away from this accursed place."

"Not so," answered Iphigenia: "I will give up my life for my father and this land of the Hellenes, and no man shall suffer for me."

And the pitiless priest led her through the throng of rude soldiers, to the grove of Artemis, wherein an altar had been built. But Achilles and Agamemnon covered their faces with their mantles, and staid inside the tent. Then Talthybius the herald stood up, and bade the warriors keep silence; and Calchas put a garland of sweet-smelling flowers about the victim's head.

"Let no man touch me," said the maiden, "for I offer my neck to the sword with right good will, that so my father may live and prosper."

In silence and great awe, the warriors stood around, while Calchas drew a sharp knife from its scabbard. But, lo! as he struck, the maiden was not there; and in her stead, a noble deer lay dying on the altar. Then the old soothsayer cried out in triumphant tones, "See now, ye men of Hellas how the gods have provided for you a sacrifice, and saved the innocent daughter of the king!" And all the people shouted with joy; and in that self-same hour, a strong breeze came down the Euripus, and filled the idle sails of the waiting ships.

"To Troy! to Troy!" cried the Hellenes; and every man hastened aboard his vessel.

How it was that fair Iphigenia escaped the knife; by whom she was saved, or whither she went,—no one knew. Some say that Artemis carried her away to the land of the Taurians, where she had a temple and an altar; and that, long years afterward, her brother Orestes found her there, and bore her back to her girlhood's home, even to Mycenæ. But whether this be true or not, I know that there have been maidens as noble, as loving, as innocent as she, who have given up their lives in order to make this world a purer and happier place in which to live; and these are not dead, but live in the grateful memories of those whom they loved and saved.

ADVENTURE XXI

THE LONG SIEGE

THE great fleet sailed once more across the sea, piloted now by Telephus, the king of Mysia; and the ships of Achilles and those of Philoctetes of Melibœa led all the rest. When they had put a little more than half the distance behind them, they came to the isle of Chryse, where were a fair temple and altars built in honor of Athené. Here many of the heroes landed; and while some were busied in refilling the water-casks from the springs of fresh water near the shore, others went up to the temple and offered gifts and heart-felt thanks to Pallas Athené. But as Philoctetes, the cunning archer, stood near one of the altars, a water-snake came out of the rocks and bit him on the foot. Terrible, indeed, was the wound, and great were the hero's sufferings; day and night he groaned and cried aloud by reason of the bitter pain; and there was no physician that could heal him of the grievous hurt. In a few days, a noisome stench began to issue from the wound, and the hero's complainings waxed so loud and piteous that the warriors stopped their ears, so that they might not hear them. Then the chiefs took counsel as to what it were best to do with him; and, although some advised that he be cast into the sea, it was thought best to follow a milder course, and leave him alone on the isle of Lemnos. Hence, while the hero slept, Odysseus and his men carried him on shore; and they laid his great bow, even the bow of Heracles, by his side upon the sand, and put a cask of water and a basket of food within easy reach of his hand. Then they sailed away, and left him alone in his great distress and sorrow.

At length the shores of Ilios were reached, and the high towers of Troy were seen. Then the sails of the vessels were furled and laid away in the roomy holds, the masts were lowered with speed, and the oarsmen seated themselves upon the benches and rowed the ships forward until they stood in one line, stretching more than a league along the shore. But as they drew nearer the sea-beach, the heroes saw all the plain before them covered with armed men, and horses and chariots drawn up to hinder their landing. And they paused, uncertain what to do; for Calchas the soothsayer had declared that he who should first step foot upon the shores of Ilios should meet a sudden death.

"Who among all the heroes will dare be the first to die for Hellas?" was the anxious question heard on every vessel. Not a man was there who was not willing and ready to be the second one to step on shore; but who would be the first? The Trojan host now began to shoot their arrows toward the ships, and to taunt the Hellenes with cowardice. Yet even Achilles and Ajax Telamon, the mightiest of the heroes, fell back and would not take the fearful risk of beginning the fight. Then Protesilaus, who had led forty black ships from Phylace and the shore of Antrona, seeing that some one must die for the cause, leaped boldly out of the ship upon the shelving beach. At once a hundred arrows whistled through the air, and glanced from his sevenfold shield of ox-hide; and a heavy spear, thrown by Hector, the mightiest of the Trojans, pierced his fair armor, and laid him bleeding and dead upon the sand. Quickly the warriors leaped ashore; face to face and hand to hand they fought with the Trojan host; and, led by Achilles and by Diomede of the loud war-cry, they drove their foes across the plain and even through the city gates.

But Protesilaus lay dead upon the beach; and few of the heroes remembered that to him they owed their victory. And when his newly-wedded wife, fair Laodamia, heard in far Phylace that he had fallen first in the fight, she dight herself in mourning and went to pray at the shrine of mighty Zeus. And the prayer which she offered was that she might see her husband once again, and holding his hand, might talk with him if it were only for the space of three hours. Then Hermes led the war-loving hero back to the upper world; and he sat in his bridal chamber, and spoke sweet words of comfort to Laodamia. But when the short hours were past, and the messenger came to lead Protesilaus back to the land of shades, his wife prayed that she might return with him. And men say that this prayer, also, was heard, and that arm in arm the two went forth together to their shadowy home in Hades.

Time would fail me to tell you how the Greeks encamped upon the plain of Troy, and how for more than nine long years they laid siege to that great city. Neither can I speak of the ruinous wrath of Achilles which brought so much woe upon the Hellenes; for of that you will read in the oldest and grandest poem that the world has ever known,—the Iliad of Homer. And there, also, you will read of the death of Patroclus; and of the vengeance which Achilles wrought, even by the slaying of godlike Hector; and of the mighty deeds of Diomede and of Ajax and of Agamemnon on the plains of Troy; and of the shrewd counsels and crafty schemes of Odysseus, who, though in strength surpassing other men, learned to trust rather to his skill in words than to his mastery of arms.

The time at length drew near when that which had been spoken concerning the doom of Achilles was to be fulfilled. For, when he saw that he, more than all the Hellenes, was held in dread by the Trojans, his heart was puffed up with unseemly pride, and he boasted of his deeds, and spoke of himself as greater even than Phœbus Apollo. Then the archer-god was greatly angered, and no longer covered him with his great shield of protection, but left him to his doom. Hence, on a day, when he stood before the Scæan gate, and taunted the Trojans on the walls, a mighty spear smote him, and pierced his heart. Some say that the weapon was thrown by Paris, the perfidious one who had caused this bloody war; and others say that far-darting Apollo in his wrath launched the fatal bolt. The body of Achilles incased in his glorious armor lay all day long in the dust, while Hellenes and Trojans fought around it, and neither could gain the mastery, or carry away the ghastly prize. At length a great storm burst upon the combatants: the thunder rolled, the lightning flashed, the rain and hail fell in blinding torrents; and the Trojans withdrew behind their walls. Then the Hellenes lifted the body of Achilles, and carried it to their ships; and, stripping it of his matchless armor, they laid it on a couch, and standing around it, they bewailed his untimely death. And his mother, silver-footed Thetis, came across the waves with all the sea-nymphs in her train; and, while she wept over the body of her child, the nymphs arrayed it in shining robes which they themselves had woven in their coral caves. Then, after many days and nights of bitter lamentation, the Hellenes built a great funeral pile upon the beach; and they laid the hero thereon, and set fire to it, and the flames leaped high over the sea, and Achilles was no more. Then Thetis took the hero's glorious armor, and set it up as a prize to that one who should excel in feats of strength and skill in a grand trial to be made beside the ships. Only two of all the host stood up for the trial,—Ajax Telamon and Odysseus; for no other man dared contend with either of these. Mighty indeed was the contest; but in the end Odysseus prevailed, and the matchless armor was awarded him. Then, when Ajax knew that he had been beaten in the suit,—and beaten not more by honest strength and skill than by crafty guile,—he fell prone upon the earth, and his great mind lost its balance. And when he arose to his feet, he knew no longer his friends and comrades, nor did he remember any thing. But like a roaring wild beast, he rushed from the tents into the fields and pasture lands; and, seeing a flock of sheep browsing among the herbage, he fell upon them with his sword, and slaughtered great numbers of them, fancying that they were foemen seeking his life. Nor did any man dare say any thing to him, or try in any way to check him, or turn him aside from his mad freaks. When he grew tired, at length, of slaughtering the helpless beasts, he went down into a green dell, and fell upon his own sword. A great stream of blood gushed from the wound, and dyed the earth, and from it sprang a purple flower bearing upon its edges both the initials of his name and a sign of woe, the letters αι.

Then Odysseus bewailed his comrade's unhappy death. "Would that I had never prevailed, and won that prize!" he cried. "So goodly a head hath the earth closed over for the sake of these arms, even that of Ajax, who in beauty and in feats of war was of a mould far above all other men, save only peerless Achilles. What a tower of strength wert thou! Long indeed shall it be ere Hellas shall see another like thee!"

After this the Hellenes began to despair; for many of their noblest heroes had perished. Who now should lead them on to victory? Surely not Patroclus, nor Achilles, nor Ajax. Bitter murmurings were heard among the ships, and the men declared that ere another moon should pass, they would embark and sail back to their loved homes, nor ask the leave of Agamemnon.

At the foot of Mount Ida there stood a temple of Apollo, built by the Trojans while yet sweet Peace was smiling on the land. To that temple Helenus the wise soothsayer, one of Priam's sons, was wont to go, stealing out from the city in the darkness of midnight, and returning ere the gray dawn of morning appeared. He went that he might learn from bright Apollo the secrets of the future, and he fondly hoped that his going was unknown to the foes of Troy. But shrewd Odysseus found him out; and one night, with a band of men, he lay in wait for the prophet-prince, and took him captive.

"This is a rich treasure that we have taken," said Odysseus, "and it shall repay us for all our losses."

Helenus was straightway taken to the camp. Around him gathered the heroes,—Agamemnon, Nestor, Menelaus, and all the rest,—demanding that he should uncover the secrets of the future.

"When and how shall the Hellenes overcome your city of Troy?" said Odysseus. "Tell us this, and tell us truly, or death in its fearfullest form shall come upon thee swiftly."

Then the trembling seer revealed to his enemies that which he had learned at Apollo's shrine. He told them that within the present year the Hellenes would certainly prevail if only they did three things, without which Troy could never be taken. First, the Palladion, the monster image of Athené, must be removed from the temple in the city, and set up in the camp by the seashore. Second, young Pyrrhus the son of Achilles must be brought from his island-home of Scyros to take the place of his father at the head of the Myrmidon host. And third, Philoctetes, who had been so deeply wronged by the chiefs, and left to perish on the desert shores of Lemnos, must be found and brought to Troy, and healed of his grievous wound.

"These are great tasks and heavy," said Odysseus. "Nevertheless I will undertake to see them performed."

Then he ordered a swift ship to be made ready; and with old Phoinix as companion, and a score of trusted fighting-men, he went on board, and sailed at once for Scyros the quondam home of great Achilles. Ten days afterward he returned, bringing with him the lad Pyrrhus, so like his glorious father in face and figure that the Myrmidons hailed him at once as their chief and king.

"Thus have I done one of the three tasks," said Odysseus. "I shall perform the other two, mayhap as easily, and then the high walls of Troy shall fall before us."

Pyrrhus found the hero living alone in a wretched cave with no friend but the mighty bow of Heracles, and suffering still great torments from the horrid wound in his foot. Yet the prince could not prevail upon him to sail to Troy; for he said that he would rather endure the distress, the hunger, and the loneliness which were his in Lemnos, than meet again those false friends who had left him there to die. Then Odysseus came forth from his hiding-place, with a company of men, to seize the hero and carry him by force on board the vessel. But this the young prince would not permit; and Philoctetes, when he saw them, fled into the innermost parts of his cave, and would not come forth. When Odysseus found that neither threats nor entreaties would prevail upon the hero, he went back to his ship, and made ready to return to Troy. Then it was that a vision appeared to Philoctetes,—a vision of mighty Heracles clothed in bright raiment, and a great glory shining in his face.

"Go thou to the land of Ilios," said the vision. "There thou shalt first be healed of thy grievous sickness; and afterwards thou shalt do great deeds, and shalt aid in taking the city; and the first prize of valor shall be awarded to thee among all the heroes. For it is the will of the immortals that Troy shall be taken, and that my bow shall mightily aid in its overthrow."

Then Philoctetes went forth from his hiding-place, and was taken on board the vessel. And as the sails were spread, and the breezes wafted them towards the Trojan shore, he bade a tearful farewell to Lemnos, where he had spent so many years of loneliness and sorrow:—

"Farewell to thee, O home that didst befriend me when others failed! Farewell, ye nymphs that haunt the meadows and the shore, or dwell beside the gushing mountain springs. Farewell, O cave that oft hast been my shelter from the winter's frosty winds and the sweltering rays of the summer's sun. I leave you now; and thou, O sea-girt Lemnos, I may never more behold! And grant, ye gods, that favoring winds may blow, and carry me safely wheresoe'er the Fates would have me go!"

As soon as the heroes reached the Trojan shore, and the ship was drawn to its place high on the beach, Philoctetes was carried to the tents, and given in charge of Machaon, Asclepius' noble son. And as he lay upon a cot in the tent of the kind physician, a sweet odor, like that of blossoming orchards and the bloom of clover, filled the air around him, and he slept; and men said that the spirit of Asclepius had fanned him into slumber. Then Machaon, with matchless skill, cut out the poisoned flesh from his foot, and cleansed it, and bound it up with soft linen. And when the hero awoke, the pain had left him; and the wound from which he had suffered such untold torments began at once to heal.

It chanced one day as Philoctetes was sitting outside of his tent, that a party of Trojans led by

Paris made a sally from the city gates, and came scouring across the plain, intent on doing mischief to the Hellenes. As the daring warriors drew near the tents, Philoctetes fitted an arrow to the great bow of Heracles, and took aim at their fair-faced leader. The deadly dart pierced the shoulder of Paris, and he fell headlong from his chariot; and there he would have met his death, had not his comrades quickly rallied, and carried him, faint with pain, back to the city and his father's halls. Terrible were the tortures which the hero suffered, for the arrow was one of those which Heracles had poisoned by dipping in the blood of the hydra. The venom sped through his burning veins; his strength failed him; the torments of a thousand deaths seemed to be upon him. Then he forgot fair Helen, for whose sake was all this war and bloodshed; and he bethought him of gentle Œnone, whom, in the innocent days of youth, he had wooed and won in the pleasant dales of Ida. And he cried aloud, "Bring to me Œnone, her whom I have so grievously wronged! She alone can heal me of my hurt!"

Then swift messengers were sent to the woody slopes of Ida, to find, if it might be, the long-deserted, long-forgotten wife. "Come quickly and save thy erring but repentant husband,"—such was the message,—"behold, he suffers from a grievous wound! But thou art skilled in the healing art above all who dwell in Ilios; and he prays that, forgiving all wrong, thou wilt hasten to help him."

When Œnone heard the message, she remembered the cruel wrongs which she had endured so long at the hands of faithless Paris; and without a word in answer, she turned away and went about her daily tasks in her humble cottage home. Then the messengers returned to Troy, and told the prince that Œnone would not come to help him. And Paris, with a groan of pain and a sigh of despair, turned his face to the wall, and died.

Then Œnone, too late, repented that she had turned a deaf ear to her husband's last request. And in haste she clad herself in her wedding robes, and came to the sad halls of the prince, not knowing that death had taken him. Fair and beautiful as in the days of her youth, she stood before his lifeless form. She took his cold hands in her warm palm, and said, "I have come, O Paris! Waken, and speak to me! Dost thou not remember me,—Œnone, whom thou didst woo in the flowery dells of Ida? I am still the same, and never have I wronged thee. Speak to me, O Paris!" Then she knelt beside him, and saw the gaping wound which the arrow of Philoctetes had made; and she knew that life had fled, and that the hero never more would waken or speak to her. And the gentle heart of Œnone was broken with the anguish which came upon her; and when the men of Troy laid Paris upon the funeral pile, and the smoke and flame arose towards heaven, the fair, perfidious prince was not alone, for Œnone shared his blazing couch.

While Troy was in mourning for the unhappy death of Paris, Odysseus and Diomede were planning the means by which to obtain the sacred image of Athené—the Palladion of Troy. In the guise of a ragged beggar, Odysseus found his way into the city, and to the door of the temple where the great image stood.

"Ah, Odysseus! I know thee despite thy rags!" was whispered into his ear, as a fair hand offered him a pittance. He looked up, and saw the peerless Helen before him, as beautiful as when, a score of years before, the princes of Hellas had sued for her hand at the court of old Tyndareus.

"Be not afraid," she said, "I will not betray you."

And then she told him how unhappy she had been in Troy, and how she longed to return to her countrymen and to her much-wronged husband Menelaus. And she promised to aid him in whatever way she could, to carry off the treasured Palladion, and to open the way for the overthrow of Troy. Odysseus, shrewdest of men, talked not long with the princess, but soon returned to the camp. Three nights later, he and Diomede made their way by stealth into the city, and carried away the priceless Palladion.

And now the three tasks which Helenus had spoken of, had been performed. What more remained ere the doomed city should be overthrown? The chiefs must needs again consult with shrewd Odysseus; and the plan which he proposed was carried out. A wooden horse, of wondrous size, was made; and in it the doughtiest heroes of the host, with young Pyrrhus as their leader, hid themselves. Then the rest of the Hellenes embarked, with all their goods, aboard their ships, and sailed away beyond the wooded shores of Tenedos. But the monster horse, with its hidden load of heroes, stood alone upon the beach.

When the Trojans, looking from their high towers, beheld their enemies depart, they were filled with joy; and, opening wide their gates, they poured out of the city, and crowded across the plain, anxious to see the wonderful horse,—the only relic which their foes had left upon their shores. While they were gazing upon it, and hazarding many a guess at its purpose and use, a prisoner was brought before the chiefs. It was Sinon, a young Hellene, who had been found lurking among the rocks by the shore. Trembling with pretended fear, he told the Trojans a sad, false story, of wrongs which he said he had suffered at the hands of Odysseus.

"But what meaneth this monster image of a horse? Tell us that," said the Trojan chiefs.

Then Sinon told them how the Hellenes had suffered great punishment at the hands of Athené, because they had stolen the sacred Palladion of Troy, and how it was on this account that they had at last given up the siege of Troy, and had sailed away for their homes in distant Hellas. And he told them, too, of the words of Calchas the soothsayer; that they should leave on the shores of Ilios an image which should serve the same purpose to those who honored it, as the sacred Palladion had served within the walls of Troy; and that if the Trojans should revere this figure, and set it up within their walls, it would prove a tower of strength to them, insuring eternal greatness to Troy, and utter destruction to Hellas.

Need I tell you how this artful story deceived the Trojans, and how with shouts of triumph they dragged the great image into the city? Need I tell you how, in the darkness of the night, the fleet returned from Tenedos, and the mighty host again landed upon the Trojan shore; or how the heroes, concealed within the wooden horse, came out of their hiding-place, and opened the gates to their friends outside; or how the Hellenes fell upon the astonished Trojans, awakened so suddenly from a false dream of peace; or how, with sword and torch, they slew and burned, and meted out the doom of the fated city? It was thus that the princes of Hellas performed the oath which they had sworn, years and years before, in the halls of King Tyndareus; and it was thus that the wrongs of Menelaus were avenged, fair Helen was given back to her husband, and the honor of Hellas was freed from blemish.

THE AFTER WORD

AND now, if you would learn more concerning the great heroes of the Golden Age, you must read the noble poems in which the story of their deeds is told. In the Iliad of Homer, oldest and grandest of all poems written by men, you will read of what befell the Greeks before the walls of Troy,—of the daring of Diomede; of the wisdom of Nestor; of the shrewdness of Odysseus; of the foolish pride of Agamemnon; of the nobility of Hector; of the grief of old King Priam; of the courage of Achilles. In the Æneid of Virgil, you will read of the last day of the long siege, and the fatal folly of the Trojans; of crafty Sinon; of the sad end of Laocoön, who dared suspect the object of the wooden horse; of the destruction of the mighty city; and of the wanderings of Æneas and the remnant of the Trojans until they had founded a new city on the far Lavinian shore. In the tragedies of Æschylus, you will read of the return of the heroes of Greece; of the sad death of Agamemnon in his own great banquet-hall; of the wicked career of Clytemnestra; of the terrible vengeance of Orestes; of what befell Iphigenia in Tauris, and how she returned to her native land. And in the Odyssey of Homer, second only to the Iliad in grandeur, you will read of the strange adventures of Odysseus; how he, storm-tossed and wind-driven, strove for ten weary years to return to Ithaca; how, after the fall of Troy,—

"He overcame the people of Ciconia; how he passed thence to the rich fields of the race who feed upon the lotus; what the Cyclops did, and how upon the Cyclops he avenged the death of his brave comrades, whom the wretch had piteously slaughtered and devoured; and how he came to Æolus, and found a friendly welcome, and was sent by him upon his voyage; yet 'twas not his fate to reach his native land; a tempest caught his fleet, and far across the fishy deep bore him away, lamenting bitterly. And how he landed at Telepylus, among the Læstrigonians, who destroyed his ships and warlike comrades, he alone in his black ship escaping." . . .

You will read, too, of how he was driven to land upon the coast where Circe the sorceress dwelt, and how he shrewdly dealt with her deceit and many arts:—

"And how he went to Hades' dismal realm in his good galley, to consult the soul of him of Thebes, Tiresias, and beheld all his lost comrades and his mother,—her who brought him forth, and trained him when a child; and how he heard the Sirens afterward, and how he came upon the wandering rocks, the terrible Charybdis, and the crags of Scylla,—which no man had ever passed in safety; how his comrades slew for food the oxen of the Sun; how mighty Zeus, the Thunderer, with a bolt of fire from heaven smote his swift bark; and how, his gallant crew all perished, he alone escaped with life. And how he reached Ogygia's isle, and met the nymph Calypso, who long time detained and fed him in her vaulted grot, and promised that he ne'er should die, nor know decay of age, through all the days to come; yet moved she not the purpose of his heart. And how he next through many hardships came to the Phæacians, and they welcomed him and honored him as if he were a god, and to his native country in a bark sent him with ample gifts of brass and gold and raiment."

How he made himself known to old Eumæus the swineherd, and to his son Telemachus, and how his old nurse, Eurycleia, knew him by the scar which he had received when a boy from the wild boar on Mount Parnassus. How he found his palace full of rude suitors seeking the hand of faithful Penelope; and how, with the great bow of Eurytus, he slew them all, and spared not one.

> . . . "Never shall the fame
> Of his great valor perish; and the gods
> Themselves shall frame, for those who dwell on earth,
> Sweet strains in praise of sage Penelope."

NOTES

NOTE 1.—ODYSSEUS AND HIS NURSE. *Page* 13.

IN the Odyssey, Book I., lines 425-444, a similar incident is related concerning Telemachus and Eurycleia. Many of the illustrations of life and manners given in this volume have been taken, with slight changes, from Homer. It has not been thought necessary to make distinct mention of such passages. The student of Homer will readily recognize them.

NOTE 2.—APOLLO AND THE PYTHON. *Page* 44.

Readers of the "Story of Siegfried" cannot fail to notice the resemblance of the legends relating to that hero, to some of the myths of Apollo. Siegfried, like Apollo, was the bright being whose presence dispelled the mists and the gloom of darkness. He dwelt for a time in a mysterious but blessed region far to the north. He was beneficent and kind to his friends, terrible to his foes. Apollo's favorite weapons were his silver bow and silent arrows; Siegfried's main dependence was in his sun-bright armor and his wonderful sword Balmung. Apollo slew the Python, and left it lying to enrich the earth; Siegfried slew Fafnir the dragon, and seized its treasures for his own.—See *The Story of Siegfried.*

Note 3.—Sisyphus. *Page* 51.

"Yea, and I beheld Sisyphus in strong torment, grasping a monstrous stone with both his hands. He was pressing thereat with hands and feet, and trying to roll the stone upward toward the brow of the hill. But oft as he was about to hurl it over the top, the weight would drive him back: so once again to the plain rolled the stone, the shameless thing. And he once more kept heaving and straining; and the sweat the while was pouring down his limbs, and the dust rose upwards from his head."—*Homer's Odyssey*, XI. 595.

Note 4.—A Son of Hermes. *Page* 51.

Autolycus was said to have been a son of Hermes, doubtless on account of his shrewdness and his reputation for thievery. Hermes is sometimes spoken of as the god of thieves.

Note 5.—The Choice of Heracles. *Page* 62.

This moral lesson is, of course, of much later date than that of our story. It Is the invention of the Greek sophist Prodicus, who was a contemporary of Socrates.

Note 6.—Meleager. *Page* 69.

Readers of the "The Story of Roland" will readily recognize several points of resemblance between the legend of Meleager's childhood and the story of Ogier the Dane. It is, indeed, probable that very much of the latter is simply a mediæval adaptation of the former.—See also the account of the three Norns in *The Story of Siegfried.*

Note 7.—The Death of Asclepius. *Page* 92.

The story of Balder, as related in the Norse mythology, has many points of resemblance to that of Asclepius. Balder, although a being of a higher grade than Asclepius, was the friend and benefactor of mankind. He was slain through the jealousy of the evil one: his death was bewailed by all living beings, birds, beasts, trees, and plants.—See *The Story of Siegfried.*

Note 8.—Paris and Oenone. *Page* 109

A very beautiful version of this story is to be found in Tennyson's poem entitled "Œnone." It will well repay reading.

NOTE 9.—THE SWINEHERD'S STORY. *Page* 119.

This story was afterwards related to Odysseus under very different circumstances. The curious reader is referred to the Odyssey, Book XV. 390-485.

NOTE 10.—PRAYERS. *Page* 129.

"The gods themselves are placable, though far
  Above us all in honor and in power
  And virtue. We propitiate them with vows,
  Incenses, libations, and burnt-offerings,
  And prayers for those who have offended. Prayers
  Are daughters of almighty Jupiter,—
  Lame, wrinkled, and squint-eyed,—that painfully
  Follow Misfortune's steps; but strong of limb
  And swift of foot Misfortune is, and, far
  Outstripping all, comes first to every land,
  And there wreaks evil on mankind, which Prayers
  Do afterwards redress. Whoe'er receives
  Jove's daughters reverently when they approach,
  Him willingly they aid, and to his suit
  They listen. Whosoever puts them by
  With obstinate denial, they appeal
  To Jove, the son of Saturn, and entreat
  That he will cause Misfortune to attend
  The offender's way in life, that he in turn
  May suffer evil, and be punished thus."

The Iliad (Bryant's Translation), IX. 618-636.

A sacrifice to Poseidon similar to that described here is spoken of in the Odyssey, III. 30-60.

NOTE 11.—THE LABORS OF HERCULES. *Page* 140.

It seems to have been one of the unexplainable decrees of fate, that Heracles should serve Eurystheus twelve years, and that at his bidding he should perform the most difficult undertakings. The account of the twelve labors of Heracles, undertaken by command of his master, belongs to a later age than that of Homer. The twelve labors were as follows:—

1. The fight with the Nemean lion.
2. The fight with the Lernæan hydra.
3. Capture of the Arcadian stag.
4. Destruction of the Erymanthian boar.
5. Cleansing the stables of Augeas.
6. Putting to flight the Harpies, or Stymphalian birds.
7. Capture of the Cretan bull.
8. Capture of the mares of Thracian Diomede.
9. Seizure of the girdle of the queen of the Amazons.
10. Capture of the oxen of Geryones.
11. Fetching the golden apples of the Hesperides.
12. Bringing Cerberus from the lower world.

NOTE 12. *Page* 151.

The description of the palace of Tyndareus given here has many points of resemblance to the description of the palace of Alcinous.—See *Odyssey*, VII. 85.

NOTE 13.—THE VENGEANCE OF ODYSSEUS. *Page* 224.

Palamedes, according to the ancient story, went to Troy with the heroes, where he distinguished himself by his wisdom and courage. But Odysseus, who could never forgive him, caused a captive Phrygian to write to Palamedes a letter in the name of Priam, and bribed a servant of Palamedes to conceal the letter under his master's bed. He then accused Palamedes of treachery. Upon searching the tent, the letter was found, and Palamedes was stoned to death. When Palamedes was led to death, he exclaimed, "Truth, I lament thee, for thou hast died even before me!" There are other stories as to the manner of the death of Palamedes. Some say that Odysseus and Diomede induced him to descend into a well, where they pretended they had discovered a treasure; and when he was below, they cast stones upon him, and killed him. Others state that he was drowned by them while fishing; and others that he was killed by Paris with an arrow.—See *Smith's Classical Dictionary*.

NOTE 14.—THE GARDEN OF LYCOMEDES. *Page* 230.

The curious reader may find in the description of the garden of Alcinous (Odyssey, VII. 85, *et seq.*) some resemblance to the description here given of the garden of Lycomedes.

NOTE 15.—THE CASKETS OF ZEUS. *Page* 233.

"Beside Jove's threshold stand
Two casks of gifts for man. One cask contains
The evil, one the good; and he to whom
The Thunderer gives them mingled sometimes falls
Into misfortune, and is sometimes crowned
With blessings. But the man to whom he gives
The evil only stands a mark exposed
To wrong, and, chased by grim calamity,
Wanders the teeming earth, alike unloved
by gods and men."

The Iliad, XXIV. 663-672.

NOTE 16.—DEATH OF AJAX. *Page* 257.

"The soul of Ajax, son of Telamon, alone stood apart, being still angry for the victory wherein I prevailed against him, in the suit by the ships concerning the arms of Achilles that his lady mother had set for a prize; and the sons of the Trojans made award and Pallas Athené. Would that I had never prevailed and won such a prize!"—*Odyssey*, XI. 544-548.

HELLAS,

THE SHORES OF THE ÆGEAN
AND ILIOS.

BRITISH MILES

0   10   20   30   40   50   60

Scotussa   Pasitha

Heraclea   PANGAEUS   Abdera   Dicaea
Sintica   Amphipolis   THASOS
Pella   Eion   Strymonicus S.

T H R A C I A   Syracellas

Therme   Apollonia   Acanthus
Thessalonica   Aeneia
Boraea   Alorus

Pieria   Chalc...   Olynthus   Sithonia   Athos M.

Samothrace

Dion   Torone   Pallene

Hellespontus   Abydos   Dardan...

Larissa   Oechal.   Myrina   LEMNOS   Rhoeteum   Troy

Boeotia I.   Pelion M.   TENEDOS   M Y S I A
Pelasgo...   Teuthrania   Gargara
ESSALI...   Phylace   CHRYSE   Chryse   Antandros
Scotussa   Itbrae   GERONTIA
Pharsalus   HALONNESUS   L E S B O S
Phthia   Heraclea
Cyparissus   Tyrrh...   Pergamos
Mytilene

Malis   LOCRI   Corinthus   SCYROS   Elaeus S.

Opus   Cyme

PSYRA   Erythrae   Smyrna
OKIS   B O E O T I A   Chalcis
Ozollan   Thebes   Aulis   Oropus
Bay of Crissa   Pugae   Styra   Lebedos

Marathon

Corinthus   MEGARA   ATHENS   Neapolis

Orchomenus   Mycenae   Salamis   ANDROS   SAMOS
Mantineia   ARGOS   AEGINA   CYAROS   OPHIUSSA   ICARIA
Tegea   Myconus   CYTHNOS   MYCONOS   PATMOS

HALICE   SERIRHOS   RHENEA DELOS   LEROS

PAROS

Sparta   Amy...   SIPHNOS   COS

Laistra   Helos   DONUSA   AMORGOS
Asophus   Melos   IOS   ASTYNATAE...
Epidelium   PHOLEGANDROS   SICINOS
Malea Pr.
enarum Pr.   THERA
Cythera   CYTHERA   Thera

PLATEIA

AEGILIA

INDEX TO PROPER NAMES

Alpheus, a river which flows through Arcadia and Elis.

Althea, the mother of Meleager.

Amphithea, grandmother of Odysseus.

Amphitryon, the stepfather of Heracles.

Anticleia, daughter of Autolycus, and mother of Odysseus.

Antilochus, son of Nestor.

Aphăreus, founder of the town of Arene in Messene, and father of Idas and Lynceus.

Aphrodīte, goddess of love and beauty.

Apollo, son of Zeus and Leto. He was the god of prophecy and of music and song, the punisher of evil, and the helper of men.

Arcadia, a country in the middle of the Peloponnesus.

Ares, the god of war. *Mars.*

Arethusa, a sea-nymph.

Argo, the ship upon which Jason and his companions sailed to Colchis.

Argolis, see Argos.

Argonauts, "the sailors of the Argo."

Argos, a name frequently applied by Homer to the whole of the Peloponnesus. A district north of Laconia, often called Argolis.

Argus, a monster having a hundred eyes, appointed by Here to be the guardian of Io.

Artĕmis, daughter of Zeus and Leto, and the twin-sister of Apollo. She was the goddess of the chase, and the protectress of the young and helpless. *Diana.*

Asclepius, son of Apollo, and god of the healing art. *Æsculapius.*

Atalanta, daughter of Iasus and Clymene; the fleet-footed wife of Milanion.

Athēné, goddess of wisdom, and "queen of the air;" often called Pallas Athene. *Minerva.*

Atropos, one of the Fates.

Aulis, a harbor in Bœotia, on the Euripus.

Autolycus, the grandfather of Odysseus.

Balios and Xanthos, the horses of Peleus.

Bœōtĭa, a district north of the Corinthian Gulf, bounded on the east by the Euripus, and on the west by Phocis.

Bosphŏrus, the "ox ford," the strait connecting the Sea of Marmora with the Black (Euxine) Sea.

Cadmus, a Phœnician who settled in Hellas, and founded the city of Thebes. He is said to have brought the alphabet from Phœnicia.

Calchas, the wisest soothysayer among the Hellenes. He died of grief because the soothsayer Mopsus predicted things which he had not foreseen.

Calydōn, an ancient town and district of Ætolia, on the Evenus River.

Castor, twin-brother of Polydeuces.

Centaurs, an ancient race inhabiting Mount Pelion and the neighboring districts of Thessaly.

Cephallenia, a large island near Ithaca.

Charybdis, a dreadful whirlpool on the side of a narrow strait opposite Scylla.

Cheiron, a Centaur, "the wisest of men," and the teacher of the heroes.

Chryse, an island in the Ægæan Sea; also a city on the coast of Asia Minor, south of Troy.

Circe, daughter of Helios, a sorceress who lived in the island of Æœa.

Cleopatra, wife of Meleager.

Clotho, one of the Fates.

Clytemnestra, daughter of Tyndareus and Leda, and sister of Castor and Polydeuces and Helen. She was married to Agamemnon, and became the mother of Iphigenia and Orestes.

Colchis, a country of Asia, at the eastern extremity of the Black Sea.

Copāis, a lake in Bœotia.

Corinth, a city on the isthmus between the Corinthian Gulf and the Ægæan Sea.

Corycia, a nymph who lived on Mount Parnassus.

Crissa, the ancient name of the Gulf of Corinth; also the name of a town in Phocis.

Cronus, the youngest of the Titans, and the father of Zeus. *Saturn.*

Cythēra, an island off the south-western point of Laconia.

Deianeira, wife of Heracles.

Delos, the smallest of the Cyclades islands in the Ægæan Sea.

Delphi, a town on the southern slope of Mount Parnassus.

Deucălion, son of Prometheus, and father of Hellen.

Diomēde, son of Tydeus, and king of Argos.

Dodona, an ancient oracle of Hellas, situated in Epirus in a grove of oaks and beeches.

Echion, son of Autolycus.

Elis, a country on the western coast of the
      Peloponnesus, south of Achaia.

Epaphos, son of Zeus and Io.

Eris, the goddess of discord.

Erymanthus, a mountain in Arcadia.

Eubœa, the largest island of the Ægæan Sea,
      separated from Bœotia by the Euripus.

Eumæus, the swineherd of Ithaca.

Euripus, the narrow strait between Eubœa and
      Bœotia.

Eurycleia, the nurse of Odysseus and of
      Telemachus.

Eurystheus, the master of Heracles, king of Argolis.

Eurytion, king of Phthia.

Eurytion, a Centaur.

Eurytus, king of Œchalia.

Evēnus, a river in Ætolia.

Ganymēdes, the most beautiful of mortals, son of
      Tros.

Glaucus, a fisherman who became immortal by
      eating of the divine herb which Cronus had
      sown.

Gorgons, three daughters of Phorcys and Ceto.

Gray Sisters, daughters of Phorcys.

Hades, the god of the lower regions. *Pluto.*

Hēbē, the goddess of youth.

Hector, son of Priam; the chief hero of the Trojans.

Helen, daughter of Tyndareus and Leda of
      Lacedæmon, represented in mythology as the
      daughter of Zeus and Leda. "The most
      beautiful woman in the world."

Hĕlĕnus, son of Priam, soothsayer of the Trojans.

Hēlios, the god of the sun. *Sol.*

Hellas, the name which the Greeks applied to their country. *Greece.*

Hellen, son of Deucalion and Pyrrha, and ancestor of all the Hellenes.

Hephæstus, the god of fire. *Vulcan.*

Hērē, the wife of Zeus. *Juno.*

Heracles, the most celebrated of all the old heroes. *Hercules.*

Hermes, the herald of the gods, son of Zeus and Maia. *Mercury.*

Hēsĭŏne, the sister of Priam.

Hesperia, "the western land."

Hesperides, guardians of the golden apples which Earth gave to Here on her marriage day—said by some to be the daughters of Phorcys and Ceto.

Hippodameia, wife of Peirithous.

Hyllus, son of Heracles.

Hyperboreans, a people living in the far North.

Iasus, an Arcadian, father of Atalanta.

Icarius, brother of Tyndareus, and father of Penelope.

Ida, a mountain-range of Mysia in Asia Minor, east of Troy.

Idas, "the boaster," son of Aphareus, and father of Cleopatra.

Idŏmĕneus, king of Crete.

Ilios, a name applied to the district in which Troy was situated. *Ilium.*

Ilus, son of Dardanus.

Inachus, the first king of Argos.

Io, daughter of Inachus, and mother of Epaphos
from whom was descended Heracles.

Iolcos, an ancient town of Thessaly at the head of
the Pegasæan Gulf.

Iŏle, daughter of Eurytus of Œchalia, beloved by
Heracles.

Iphigenīa, daughter of Agamemnon and
Clytemnestra.

Iphitus, son of Eurytus, one of the Argonauts.

Ithaca, a small island in the Ionian Sea, the
birthplace of Odysseus.

Jason, leader of the Argonauts.

Lacedæmon, a district of Laconia in which was
situated Sparta. The name is also applied to
the town of Sparta.

Lachĕsis, one of the Fates.

Laconia, a country in the south-east of
Peloponnesus.

Laertes, king of Ithaca, father of Odysseus.

Laodamīa, daughter of Acastus, and wife of
Protesilaus.

Laŏmĕdon, king of Troy, father of Priam.

Lăpiths, a people inhabiting the country adjoining
Mount Pelion in Thessaly.

Leda, wife of Tyndareus of Lacedæmon.

Lemnos, an island in the Ægæan Sea.

Lichas, the herald of Heracles.

Linus, a musician, brother of Orpheus.

Lycomēdes, king of Scyros.

Lydia, a district of Asia Minor.

Lynceus, son of Aphareus, brother of Idas.

Machāon, son of Asclepius, the surgeon of the Greeks in the Trojan war.

Medēa, daughter of Æétes, king of Colchis, celebrated for her skill in magic.

Medusa, one of the Gorgons.

Meleāger, son of Oineus and Althea, husband of Cleopatra.

Menelāus, brother of Agamemnon, and husband of Helen.

Messēne, a country in the south-western part of the Peloponnesus.

Milanion, the husband of Atalanta.

Mycēnæ, an ancient town in Argolis.

Mysia, a country in Asia Minor.

Nedon, a river of Messene.

Nēleus, son of Poseidon and Tyro, brother of Pelias, and father of Nestor.

Nessus, a Centaur, ferryman at the River Evenus.

Nestor, king of Pylos, son of Neleus.

Nireus, one of the heroes of the Trojan war.

Ocĕănus, god of the Ocean.

Odysseus, the hero of this story, son of Laertes, husband of Penelope. *Ulysses.*

Œchālia, a town supposed to be somewhere in Eubœa.

Œnōne, daughter of the river-god Cebren, and wife of Paris.

Œta, a rugged pile of mountains in the south of Thessaly.

Oineus, king of Pleuron and Calydon.

Olympus, a mountain in Thessaly, on the summit of which Zeus held his court.

Omphalé, a queen of Lydia.

Orestes, son of Agamemnon.

Orpheus, the greatest of the old musicians.

Orsilochus, son of Alpheus, king of Messene.

Ortygia, an island near the coast of Sicily.

Palamēdes, son of Nauplius, king of Eubœa.

Pallas Athene, see Athene.

Paris, son of Priam of Troy.

Parnassus, a mountain, or group of mountains, a few miles north of the Corinthian Gulf.

Patrŏclus, the friend of Achilles.

Peirĭthŏus, king of the Lapiths, son of Ixion and Dia.

Pēleus, son of Æacus and Endeis the daughter of Cheiron.

Pĕlĭas, son of Poseidon and Tyro, and brother of Neleus. He made himself king of Iolcos, by excluding his half-brother Æson from the throne.

Pēlĭon, a lofty mountain in Thessaly not far from Iolcos.

Peloponnesus, all that part of Hellas south of the Corinthian Gulf (Bay of Crissa).

Pĕnĕlōpē, daughter of Icarius, cousin of Helen, and wife of Odysseus.

Perseus, one of the older heroes, son of Zeus and Danaë.

Phăĕthon, son of Helios and Clymene.

Phēmius, a celebrated minstrel.

Pherae, or **Pharæ**, an ancient town in Messene on the river Nedon. Also, a town in Thessaly of which Admetus was king.

Philoctētes, a friend of Heracles, and the most celebrated archer in the Trojan war.

Phorcys, "the old man of the sea."

Phthia, a district in the south-east of Thessaly.

Polydeuces, brother of Castor and Helen. *Pollux.*

Poseidon, the god of the sea. *Neptune.*

Priam, the last king of Troy, son of Laomedon, and father of Hector and Paris.

Promētheus, a Titan, son of Iapetus, the friend of man.

Protesilāus, a hero from Phylace in Thessaly.

Proteus, the prophetic shepherd of the sea.

Pylos, a town on the south-west coast of Messene.

Pyrrha, the wife of Deucalion.

Pyrrhus, the son of Achilles, also called Neoptolemus.

Pythia, a name applied to the priestess of Apollo at Delphi.

Rhadamanthus, son of Zeus and Europa, and judge and ruler in the Islands of the Blest.

Scandia, a harbor in Cythera.

Scylla, a monster with six heads, which guarded one side of a narrow strait.

Scyros, a small island east of Eubœa.

Sinon, a grandson of Autolycus, and cousin of Odysseus.

Sisyphus, son of Ælus. He is said to have built the town of Ephyra, afterward Corinth.

Sparta, see Lacedæmon.

Stymphālus, a town in the north-east of Arcadia.

Syma, a small island off the south-western coast of Caria in Asia Minor.

Syria, or Syra, one of the Cyclades islands.

Talthybius, the herald of Agamemnon.

Tāygĕtes, a lofty range of mountains between Laconia and Messene.

Tĕlămŏn, son of Æacus and Endeis, and brother of Peleus, king of Salamis. He was the father of Ajax by Peribœa, his second wife; after the death of Peribœa, he married Hesione, the sister of Priam.

Tēlĕmăchus, the son of Odysseus and Penelope.

Telephus, son of Heracles and Auge, and king of Mysia.

Theseus, the great hero of Attica, and king of Athens.

Thessaly, the largest division of Hellas.

Thetis, a sea-nymph, wife of Peleus, and mother of Achilles.

Tilphussa, a nymph dwelling at Lake Copais.

Tiryns, a city in Argolis, not far from Mycenæ.

Trāchis, a town of Thessaly.

Trophonius, one of the architects of the temple at Delphi.

Tyndărĕus, king of Lacedæmon.

Zacynthus, an island west of Messene.

Zeus, son of Cronus, "the ruler of gods and men." *Jupiter.*

www.ingramcontent.com/pod-product-compliance
Lightning Source LLC
Chambersburg PA
CBHW031826090426
42741CB00005B/153